# I AM A SHULAMITE

## DISCOVERING DEEP FRIENDSHIP WITH THE KING OF KINGS

*By Rhonda Michelle Smith*

ISBN 979-8-9922578-2-3

Printed in the United States of America



Book Cover Design by Rhonda Michelle Smith

Edited by Heather Smith

# Contents

**Chapter 1:** *Song of Songs 1* 1

**Chapter 2:** *Song of Songs 2* 23

**Chapter 3:** *Song of Songs 3* 43

**Chapter 4:** *Song of Songs 4* 55

**Chapter 5:** *Song of Songs 5* 65

**Chapter 6:** *Song of Songs 6* 75

**Chapter 7:** *Song of Songs 7* 93

**Chapter 8:** *Song of Songs 8* 101

## Thank You!

Thank You, beloved Jesus. I never dreamed You could fill my heart with such satisfaction. I am forever Your garden locked and Your fountain sealed. As for my vineyard of love, I give it all to You forever *(Song of Solomon 8:12 TPT).*

## A Word to Brides and Sons

Men are brides and women are sons. The Bible is full of metaphors where God uses ordinary things, in which we are familiar, to describe the kingdom of heaven, which is quite extraordinary.

A healthy father-son relationship should include a son who adores his father and wishes to follow his every guidance. The son knows that the father is leading him with love and into more satisfying places in his life than he could ever have found on his own.

A bride partners with her faithful husband. She receives the invitations of her bridegroom to join him in endeavors that will not just satisfy the love they have between them, but they will change the world around them. Men and women alike would do well to walk as sons and brides with the living God.

In the first edition of this book, the cover as well as other aspects of the book drew the attention of mostly women. This new edition attempts to entice male and female alike. Within these pages, you will discover a journey that brings you into deep friendship with Jesus. Friendship is an essential first step to a healthy marriage. No different is our marriage to The One who paid the dowry price of His life for us.

I pray the revelations within these pages would open your heart and help you see your own journey with the King of kings. I pray that your love story with the Father, from whom the whole family in heaven and earth is named (Ephesians 3:14), would be revealed. And I also pray that intimate friendship would deepen with Jesus, the faithful Bridegroom who gave all, that we might be equally yoked with Him. (2 Corinthians 3:18, Romans 8:29)

Sincerely His,
Rhonda

# Introduction

I am a Shulamite. If you are on a journey with King Jesus, you are a Shulamite. Lay down preconceived thoughts of this intriguing book of the Bible, and allow me to lay down my testimony into the framework of the most beautiful love song ever written. My prayer is that, as you read my testimony in this context, you will see your own story unfold. For perhaps you too have held the hand of the King of Kings and allowed Him to draw you into a deeper relationship with Him. I pray also that you will see that your love story with Him is not complete. For all of our lives, we will be allowing Him into more of our hearts, surrendering even our deepest hidden places to Him, and allowing Him to bring healing and speak the truth. Then, our story continues on into eternity where the beauty we have allowed Him to create within us is exquisitely perfected in a realm where there is no enemy to question our identity or battle us with hurts and lies.

The Savior we fixed our eyes upon in the midst of the war on earth is now the focus of our everlasting gaze of pure love. I will be released to love Him fully as He has always loved me *(1 Corinthians 13:12)*. The One whose arms we sought for peace and comfort during the trials will hold us in unhindered rest and communion. We can even see glimpses now of beholding Him, a mesmerizing stare at such beauty that cannot be found on this earth. This gaze we return to Him, as He is constantly and passionately looking upon us, spilling first love into our being and putting all else in the dim foreground of His greatness. I once was lost in the deception of the world, trying to cover my deep rejection and replenish the love that kept slipping out of my soul as fast as the world could put its temporary satisfaction within. I was trying to climb a slippery mountain without hope, even after being introduced to and receiving Jesus. I am now found by a King who has ravished my heart because He is humble enough to say that I first ravished His *(Song of Solomon 4:9)*. In this book, I have laid out the Song of Solomon verse by verse or groups of verses together. I recommend prayerfully reading one section at a time. Allow my story and revelation to usher you into uncovering your own journey and conversation with Jesus. Use the questions or activity at the end of each section to pursue your own encounter with the King of Kings. You may want your own journal to write what the King whispers to your heart. Take time to enjoy His presence, and allow Him to enjoy you.

Jesus, may this book tell a story to glorify Your name. I was lost, but now I am found. I was deceived, but now I rest in truth. I was dry, but You made me into a well. I was buried in ash, but You drew me up into beauty. I was gasping for breath, but You gave me Your very breath. I could not feel the victory for which You paid, but You took down the embattlements and replaced them with a royal robe. Thank you, Jesus, that I have eternity to give You thanks.

## Beloved, Come

*Blessed is he*
*Who is not offended by Me*
*But come sit on my knee*
*And I will share My mysteries*
*With this child of Mine*
*Who abides as the vine.*
*This world sometimes shakes*
*And lives we've built might break.*
*Beloved, come.*

*Incline your ear*
*And you will hear.*
*Lean into Me*
*And you will see*
*I bear your burdens and your cares.*
*If I know your number of hairs,*
*Don't I know where the enemy strikes*
*And your deepest needs alike?*
*Beloved, come.*

*I honor thee.*
*I lift my eyes to see*
*The wonders of Your majesty.*
*Your goodness flows*
*And goes*
*In places some don't know*
*To lift the meek*
*And those who seek*
*Your face.*
*Beloved, come.*

*I had my eyes to the dirt*
*Not aware of my worth,*
*Searching for it in the earth,*
*But You came near*
*And whispered in my ear*
*That You'd always be here.*
*You caused my head to rise*
*And gave me dove's eyes*
*And a ring.*
*Beloved, come.*

*"The Song of Songs, which is Solomon's."*
*Song of Solomon 1:1*

Do not skip over this very first verse, beloved. Every word in scripture has a purpose, and we must be kings and queens who glory in seeking out God's treasures *(Proverbs 25:2)*. This is where we walk along the path with Him and discover truths deep in His heart which many times reveal what is in ours. How my heart has been saddened when I search for commentary on the Song of Solomon to find believers recommending their brothers to skip this book or suggesting to read it only as a book for married couples.

Most certainly this world is full of twists of God's truths, purposes, and intentions. Intimacy has been associated with shame and has been abused in some of the most heinous ways. We read some of the context in the Song of Solomon and our mind goes immediately to defense mode. As believers shielding ourselves from worldly sin, we force ourselves on the straight and narrow of religion. Most certainly it is healthy and commanded to avoid sin, but how detrimental when we run from exploring the word of God because we have a fear of falling into sin. Hebrews 10 compares the sacrificing of animals under the law to Christ's final sacrifice. Christ's perfect sacrifice wiped away sin so that we are not conscious of sin in our daily lives, being free to walk toward Him, away from willful sin and into the freedom of childlike faith and communion with our Father *(Hebrews 10:2)*. Romans 6:6 also says, *"We know that our old self was crucified with him in order that the body of sin might be brought to nothing, so that we would no longer be enslaved to sin."*

You are free to seek deeper treasures of intimacy with Jesus, the first born among many brothers *(Romans 8:29)*. In childlikeness, explore His heart for you so that you may see your true heart that was created for Him.

Digging into this first scripture of the book, the name Solomon comes from the Hebrew root salom (Strongs H7965) which we recognize as shalom and means peace. In fact, the name Shulamite derives from a similar word salam (Strongs H7999) or shalam which means to be safe or completed. It can also mean to reciprocate, which we will consider later. This beautiful book of the Bible is the story of Jesus's walk with His bride to beautify her, to show her who she truly is, to even train her so that she can see the grand purpose and calling for which He created her. This is where she will find her peace, looking at the One who is peace.

In this journey, the labels and distorted thinking of ourselves will have to succumb to a God who knows our true value. At times the chains will melt away, and at other times, we have to give Him permission to pry our unwilling fingers off of them, but in the end, the lenses of the enemy will be destroyed and we will see more clearly ourselves and the God who made us out of the pure love and intention of a perfect Father. In Him, we will truly find safety and completion, not that which is chanted over and over in hopes that our hearts and mind will experience its reality (though I do not want to discount declaration of God's word), but a tangible reality in our soul that declares for us who He is because we have walked with Him and seen His faithfulness. We have a testimony that combats any lie. We have His nature concreted in our heart and feeding truth to our mind, continually reminding us, and we have the ongoing journey with Him who never leaves us, a constant reminder of His promises.

*"Let him kiss me with the kisses of his mouth"*
*Song of Solomon 1:2a*

I love to look up original words in Hebrew and Greek to give me deeper revelation into the original authors' intentions and, more importantly, God's intentions for that scripture. You may notice an H followed by some numbers in parenthesis next to the mention of a Hebrew word. You may use this number to look up that word in the Strong's Dictionary to dive more into that word for yourself. This verse above, however, is quite important to soak in first.

Let God comfort your heart in allowing Him to tenderly kiss your forehead or your cheek as a loving father would show affection for His son or daughter. Allow the Holy Spirit to kiss your heart, imparting His affection for you and depositing value into your soul. Solomon lovingly calls the Shulamite 'his sister, his spouse, and his love' five times in this book. We know the church is the bride of Jesus, but do we individually see ourselves as His bride? He is the exalted Bridegroom who resides closely within our hearts. So high yet so close. Give Him permission to draw near, to touch the places you have shielded for so long. Give Him the weariness of carrying hurts He never meant for us to experience but because of the brokenness of this world, they were forced upon us, many times as children.

When I was perhaps between the ages of 4-7, my grandfather sexually abused me. I loved my grandfather so much. I loved his attention and adoration. I was too young to comprehend the corruption in our relationship. My instincts seemed to alert me, but I had no action to follow, no defenses to stop what I could not understand. Consequently, I was also subjected to spiritual warfare that my soul was not equipped nor mature enough to fight. I began to feel, understandably, insecure at being exposed to such mature experiences and a bit embarrassed about not understanding how to please in this way.

Of course, I now see how ridiculous it would be for a child to know such things, but a child would not. So, the enemy took full advantage to plant many lies about my own value and worth. I must lay down in forgiveness for all that happened in the midst of my grandfather's brokenness. He made choices to deal with his own pain that were unacceptable, but I must allow my heavenly Father to be my vindicator. I cannot lay claim to gaining my own retribution. One of the very first acts of obedience as a new believer, even before I was fully aware of hearing God's voice, was to forgive these unthinkable crimes that had been committed against me. I remember struggling with that single act for well over a year, thinking about it frequently but just not having the strength to do it. Thankfully I had the will to do it. I remember my beloved grandmother passing and her grave being placed, at her request, right next to his, joined by a headstone. I hated this fact and did not understand why someone I saw as so precious could agree to be near someone so wretched.

When I was about nine, I remember seeing my grandfather in the kitchen with the local pastor, sitting on chairs, talking as I had never seen him converse with anyone else before. Most of my memories of him were of him in bed or sitting on the side of his bed, ridden with a back injury. The family would go in to acknowledge him or my grandmother would take him coffee with honey or regular meals. As he sat with the preacher that evening, my mind processed the thought that he certainly should be sitting with a pastor after all he's done, trying to get right. My thoughts were not of beautiful surrender to God but of scrambling to do something to make up for the offenses he had so easily handed out to me and others in our family.

Now as an adult attempting to forgive, I finally told God that if He wanted me to forgive him, He would have to help me. I don't remember the moment I forgave my grandfather, but I remember thinking about him one day and the sting was gone. The memories were not as graphic, and pain had been released. I graciously thanked the Lord for His kindness that seemed to come into the night and steal away the dark. This is when my heart consciously began to allow the Lord to kiss my heart, to allow Him to begin to pour in goodness, supernatural goodness I had not yet felt. I had seen His faithfulness in my surrender. I felt the freedom that His beautiful ways could offer, and I thirsted for more. I spent many years without following Jesus, trying to search the world to heal a hurt that I didn't yet know I had. I said many times of my abuse, "I'm so glad it has not affected me at all," but I said that amidst many harmful life patterns that I considered to be my own choices to live free. Now I know His love is better than the wine of the world. He never brings up hurtful pasts without leading us into healed futures.

With fresh freedom in hand to allow the kisses of our Father, we can look deeper. The verb kiss and the noun kisses both derive from the root word nasaq (H5401) which means to equip with weapons. When we feel the unconditional love of a good father, we are equipped to conquer. Have you ever had a good friend cheering you on to do something difficult? Their encouragement may mean the difference between you following through or not. Knowing who He created you to be and who you are in Him, fully loved and accepted, encourages you to reach out and grab the destiny He has for you, to walk out all the pages in your book He has written for you *(Psalm 139:16)*. *"In all these things we are more than conquerors through him who loved us" (Romans 8:37)*. Beloved, you are a conqueror, and more, because you have joined with His great love for you! The more you allow yourself to receive the love He is pouring out to you, the more you receive sonship/daughtership and walk in who you truly are. One of His favorite things to do is tell you who you are in the righteousness that is yours through His love.

**ACTIVATION:**

Holy Spirit, is there anyone I need to forgive so that my heart can be softened to encounter you more fully?

---

*"For your love is better than wine; your anointing oils are fragrant; your name is oil poured out; therefore virgins love you" Song of Solomon 1:2b-3*

His affection toward us is better than anything the world offers to ease the pain or give us value. The word wine (H3196) infers bubbling over or a banquet. There is a kind of abundance in the world. We all have made choices to partner with the world to fill our needs. We may numb the pain with drugs or entertainment or seek recognition through our job so we feel important, as well as countless other ways to avoid pain and enjoy life. We have a deep need to walk in the cool of the day with acceptance and every other need met. However, when we start consulting God about His plans for us, we begin to seek His anointing on our lives that turns what we are doing on the earth into partnering with heaven. Sometimes that looks like a career change, and sometimes it is simply a change in our point of view in our current circumstances.

David was a shepherd who did what he had to do to keep his father's sheep well, including rescuing them from the mouths of lions and bears, but God was preparing him for bold leadership to shepherd Israel. David had smelled the fragrant anointing of his calling when Samuel physically poured the oil on his head, and a new level of boldness arose to conquer an enemy, Goliath, no other trained warrior dared to fight. God told David who he was, and David walked out the calling with training in hand that he had received in the field.

One of my favorite jobs during motherhood was working at my children's preschool. I had been there several years, and parents began to request my class for their children. I enjoyed the creativity allowed as well as the difference I felt I was making in the lives of the children and their families. One summer as the new year approached, I heard the Lord tell me my time was up there. I hesitated at this word, not only because I loved the job but I also had no other job lined up. I had volunteered for a ministry that summer, and they had invited me out of town the same week I was to do annual training with the preschool. I left the job I loved, and I soon after struggled with my identity and purpose. I enjoyed the ministry but did not see it as a home for me. The Lord told me He was building a new identity in me, one that was rooted in Him. As He poured His value into me, the fragrant oil, I could more boldly move forward in the new things He had for me, and I began to see the job at the preschool was training me in my current ministry praying with others to help align their hearts and their families' hearts with the kingdom of God.

Jesus's name, which is the fullness of His character, the name that represents all of who He is, was poured out for us to be able to rise up as His bride, carrying all His authority. There is nothing He has not provided us unto life and godliness, through knowing Him who has called us to glory and virtue (2 Peter 1:3). Do you see an anointing God has poured on you in the form of a gifting or talent? Don't overlook jobs, hobbies, or characteristics that are easy for you. They do not come easy to everyone. The anointing prophesies who God created you to be.

You are no longer in the chamber of the world, but He has brought you into His chambers *(Song of Solomon 1:4)*, into the many rooms of the Father *(John 14:2)* where you have full access to the inheritance being a child of the King.

**ACTIVATION:**

Jesus, show me my strengths and talents that you have given me so I may begin taking steps toward my purpose, partnering with You.

*"I am very dark, but lovely, O daughters of Jerusalem, like the tents of Kedar, like the curtains of Solomon. Do not gaze upon me because I am dark, because the sun has looked upon me. My mother's sons were angry with me; they made me keeper of the vineyards, but my own vineyard I have not kept!"*
*Song of Solomon 1:5-6*

Inside our hearts, a shadow can loom, sometimes consciously known but other times buried underneath religious effort or below masks to present ourselves as acceptable. This is the shadow of shame and condemnation for past choices or coping strategies we use to ease the pain of feeling lack or defeat in our lives. Tents and curtains are used for barriers. They are put in place to hide or protect. At our initial salvation, Jesus has come in to make our spirit righteous (Romans 8:3-4), so we are, in fact, lovely. The original word "lovely" (H5000) could be translated as "appropriate." When we receive Jesus, we are now made appropriate to live in communion with Him. Just as praise is appropriate to sing to God *(Psalm 33:1, 147:1)*, we are in an appropriate position when we stand before Him fully accepted, covered in the full payment of Jesus. However, even with this victory, our hearts can feel less than victorious. Although our spirit is made perfect at initial salvation, our soul must be healed and renewed to live in what our spirit is experiencing.

At a young age, when I was abused sexually by my grandfather, a cycle of insecurity and rejection began within me. While in school, I had friends but never felt fully accepted. As I grew, I began to seek acceptance from boys, and in early adulthood, I chose nude dancing as a way to receive the acceptance my heart desperately needed. All the world offers is a depreciating commodity. Where I found a degree of acceptance, it was never enough, and I had to seek further measures of it to keep my heart feeling satiated. Even after leaving the night job and saying yes to Jesus life, I stayed in patterns of filling my heart with the world, just in more socially acceptable methods. I began to try to arrange my family into the perfect appearance toward the outside, believing I was doing all for their good. I had expectations on them they couldn't reach.

I served at my church, which, with the correct heart motive, is healthy, but subconsciously my motive was approval and acceptance from my peers. This spilled into every aspect of my life, always trying to prove my value that was already settled at the cross.

During a prayer session, Jesus gave me a vision to deal with the identity crisis my heart was trying to cover. In the vision, I saw myself in a revealing dress I would have never worn in this new season of my life, and Jesus appeared next to me on a stage I knew from the dancing job, causing a surge of tears to flow. I could not accept, at first, that Jesus would meet me in this place where my identity seemed to be trapped in shame and condemnation. Immediately, my inappropriate dress became a bridal gown and Jesus was dressed in Prince Charming attire.

I then looked out to the dirty surroundings beyond the stage, the men staring and darkness looming. Jesus pulled a curtain across the front of the stage, and we began to dance as a couple taking their first steps in harmony together. My heart began to release as my steps followed His. The curtain opened and revealed what seemed like the same tables, the same building but transformed into gold where couples in formal attire sat and smiled upon our dance.

My Prince Jesus walked me down off the stage, arm in arm. As we walked to the door I noticed a man wearing a tuxedo in an upper seating area. I recognized him as a man who had touched me during my time as a dancer, and afterward, I slapped him pretty hard. He had asked several times if he could touch me, and I had denied him. As I walked past, I freely forgave him; then, flashes of faces came before me of bouncers, deejays, managers, and other men who should have protected me but actually encouraged me in hiring myself out for profit. "I forgive you!" I cried out over and over until the faces ceased. Jesus and I walked out of that building, and I left with a new revelation of my identity.

Many of "your mother's sons", believers and unbelievers, will allow and even put you in positions that benefit them but might bury you. At first, unhealthy positions might not feel like burying or even like work. They feel like they are filling a need within you, but as their ability to fill depreciates, you find yourself working their vineyard. We might stay there, getting exhausted, and eventually leave, many times with bitterness and the feeling of being used.

**ACTIVATION:**

Ask Jesus to show you the places you are trying to prove your identity and worth. Surrender your heart to be aligned to His desires for you. Use your own words to express your heart to Him.

*"Tell me, you whom my soul loves, where do you pasture your flock, where you make it lie down at noon; for why should I be like one who veils herself beside the flocks of your companions?"*
*Song of Solomon 1:7*

Working vineyards to which Jesus has called us is vital. Following our own reason can mislead us. Delight in Him, and He will give you the desires of your heart *(Psalm 37:4)*. As you delight in Jesus, seeking Him, sitting in prayer, listening and speaking to Him, and reading His Word, the desires in your heart will begin to align with His desires for you. He will pour heavenly desire into your heart, and He will fill not only these new desires but perhaps even desires that were birthed from the way He created you. He will lead you to fulfill your destiny and calling He planned for you, and He just might give you good things you simply desire because He loves to surprise and lavish His Bride!

I came out of the dancing profession not knowing who I truly was but jumped right into marriage and motherhood. I began to work the world's vineyards by attempting to mold my family into an acceptable example of superficial success. There is nothing wrong with success in the world and having a life that appears and is desirable as long as that life is in partnership with Jesus. Living our best is a counterfeit and is less than subpar to a life that is His best for us.

He has planned more than we can think or imagine for us which means our wildest dreams for ourselves cannot comprehend His dreams for us. Tell me, Jesus, where do you bring me into this kind of partnership and rest in You? We get weary of veiling ourselves around others, trying to be someone we truly are not. Do not forget, beloved, the Bridegroom in verse 1 lifts the veil of His bride to kiss her. When you allow the washing of His words over you to cleanse untrue thoughts about yourself from your heart, you are no longer ashamed and stand with your head up as the one whom His soul loves!

**ACTIVATION:**

Jesus, speak words to me right now of how you see me, coming against any hidden lies I may believe about myself.

*"If you do not know, O most beautiful among women, follow in the tracks of the flock, and pasture your young goats beside the shepherds' tents. I compare you, my love, to a mare among Pharaoh's chariots. Your cheeks are lovely with ornaments, your neck with strings of jewels."Song of Solomon 1:8-10*

The journey of the Shulamite is not one to take alone. Have you ever seen someone else, and something about them intrigued you and attracted you to them? Oftentimes it's confidence, compassion, boldness, or how they encourage and lift up others. They are good leaders or they flow well in their gifts, talents, and callings. Beloved, go pasture your flock beside them for a season but do not try to take on their tent. If bad company corrupts good morals, good company can encourage us and help us rise above, but we must caution ourselves against comparing or taking from them what is not ours. Jesus sees you uniquely. If I compare myself with other gifted believers, I am setting my life and the treasure of my giftings before the enemy, allowing him to pick me apart.

The word mare (H5484) in the verse above can mean to skip joyfully. Imagine a crowd of stately horses with beautifully crafted chariots behind each one. In the center of this crowd is an exuberant mare, leaping in the excitement of her Beloved. This is how Jesus sees you! Your hunger to seek Him and grow in Him ravishes His heart, and you become more like Him who leaps for joy at His beloved's pursuit!

He has never made anyone like you; your face and your spiritual adornments are like no other combination in humanity's history. Learn from others but be yourself!

**ACTIVATION:**

Jesus, open doors to divine friendships which inspire me to be all you created me to be.

---

*"While the king was on his couch, my nard gave forth its fragrance. My beloved is to me a sachet of myrrh that lies between my breasts. My beloved is to me a cluster of henna blossoms in the vineyard of Engedi." Song of Solomon 1:12-14*

When we commune with the King, our hearts must be humble. We must recognize He has offered us a gift we cannot attain on our own. Our own humility and revelation of the greatness of His gift will grow as we see Him more and more clearly and become more aware of His nature. Did Mary read this verse before she unashamedly broke into the dinner party to pour out her thankfulness and surrender upon Jesus? She had some sort of revelation of her need and His sufficiency to which she clung tightly to her heart, the myrrh on her chest.

The first adult church I attended housed the preschool where I taught. Through several closed doors, I realized the Lord was pulling me out of that church for the next season, but I remained a teacher at the school. One morning in my quiet time, I read Proverbs 16:16-19, and the phrase "haughty eyes" was highlighted to me. The word haughty (H7311) can be translated as proud or exalting self. The Lord was gracious to show me a hurt place in my heart that I was overlooking in regards to the doors that had closed to me in that church. I had said all the right things to myself, "The Lord is just moving me on" and "There are other places He wants me to be."

However, somewhere underneath that, I was hurt and used pride to deal with the pain and was unknowingly growing an unfruitful branch in my heart. If I were honest, that might have sounded like, "I have outgrown them anyway" or "I now understand things they don't." In that morning quiet time with my Beloved King, He so gently said, "Go wash the pastors' feet." I wept at the thought. I knew I had to commit quickly by receiving their permission, or I would certainly talk myself out of it. This was a Saturday morning, and I knew even a weekend to sit on it before seeing them at preschool Monday morning would be enough time to back out.

Jesus always has His work complete in the background if we agree to see it. That very day, we had been invited to a fun gathering to which all the pastors and office staff had been also invited. Catching two of the three pastors alone in the kitchen, I asked if I could wash their feet after service the following Sunday. I know they must have been surprised and maybe baffled at my quick request, but after they acquiesced, I hurried off, not waiting for further discussion. I attended church services at their church, weeping through the entire service, the Holy Spirit active in my heart and mind, no doubt preparing me for the healing that I was to receive.

I laid out my basins of water and towels for each of them, and as I draped water over their feet I prayed for each one, tears flowing freely. I told them I realized I had haughty eyes that were displeasing to the Lord and asked forgiveness. Each pastor in turn prayed for me as well. Afterward, when I saw that church building, either for work or in passing, I realized a thorn had been taken. There was a new fondness that swept over me at each glance and at the thought of each person and family that had contributed to my growth while I had been there. Later, one pastor came to me and told me he was teaching a bible study of Mary's sacrifice to Jesus at His feet. He told me that there was a deeper understanding of that story after the pouring out in that church office. I imagine he has been at least a little changed after that, too. Isn't that like Jesus? He does more than we can each comprehend and touches us in ways we cannot predict. We pour forth a fragrance to honor Him, and yet we have a fragrance of Him to pull close to us as well. That vineyard of the world that once ruled over us is now His vineyard that is a delight to enjoy.

**ACTIVATION:**

Jesus, show me any branch not bearing fruit in my heart that I may allow you to prune. Show me any unforgiveness or judgment weighing me down, even hidden, that you wish to carry for me today.

---

*"Behold, you are beautiful, my love; behold, you are beautiful; your eyes are doves. Behold, you are beautiful, my beloved, truly delightful. Our couch is green; the beams of our house are cedar; our rafters are pine." Song of Solomon 1:15-17*

Do you realize, beloved, that your dwelling place goes from His chambers in verse 4 to "our house" in verse 17? How could the King of Glory allow me to lay claim to a house that is clearly His? It's His goodness, and honestly, that house has been yours since salvation but it took maturity and growth to see it. We see it when we train our hearts to become more singularly focused on the truths of heaven and allow the lies of the enemy to fall.

He says her eyes are like doves eyes. Doves remain monogamous in their mating season, so when we have doves' eyes, we are faithful to not only see Jesus for who He truly is as we continually gaze upon Him, but we see our reflection in His eyes, the way He sees us as well. Ask Jesus to give you a vision of how He sees you. Don't allow your own thoughts of yourself to intercept. In football, the opposing team steals the ball for an interception so that they can carry the ball and score. If you allow yourself to intercept what Jesus says about you, you are allowing the enemy to steal thoughts Jesus is trying to gift you to grow you and grow His kingdom.

**ACTIVATION:**

Show me a vision of how You see me, Jesus.

*"I am a rose of Sharon, a lily of the valleys. [He says] As a lily among brambles, so is my young love among the young women."*
*Song of Solomon 2:1*

Commentators have different points of view on just who is the rose and the lily. Is it the king or the Shulamite? Most ascribe it to the king. I cannot disagree, but I have encountered Him as the One who says that I am the rose. Consider the parable of the pearl of great price.

*"Again, the kingdom of heaven is like a merchant in search of fine pearls, who, upon finding one pearl of great value, went and sold all he had and bought it" (Matthew 13:45-46).*

When most read this for the first time, we see Jesus as the pearl that we must surrender everything to purchase. Certainly, He is worth all we possess. However, in our humanity, can we surrender all in our possession unless we have felt the reality of the other person's allegiance? If our heart hesitates to give all, our words of surrender are, at best, well-meaning chants attempting deeper faith in our own strength, and, at worst, simply empty words. The cross is not a story to which we simply concede but an experience that Jesus accomplished to open the veil for us to experience in our hearts and minds. Conceding rather than experiencing is like being a royal son who walks into the foyer of his father's home and refuses to go any farther. When we see that our King has surrendered all to us first, that He sees great value in who He created, and that He considers us worth His very life to purchase a relationship with us, then our hearts are melted like wax at the feet of such a generous King. If we refuse to acknowledge our value and worth to Him, we are dishonoring the Creator; for who scoffs at a creation yet attempts to honor the One who created? If you can see yourself as the pearl, then you can truly see Him as the pearl.

The Holy Spirit says through Paul in Romans 12:10, *"Love one another with brotherly affection. Outdo one another in showing honor."* Jesus says in Matthew 23:11, *"The greatest among you shall be your servant."*

God does not call us to do anything that He has not done first. Jesus is the greatest who has ever walked among us, and He says that He is our servant. He also loved us first. He is so secure in

Himself that He never fears championing us and putting us first. We become like Him when we also do this. His nature never changes. He is still putting us first today in order that our hearts might succumb to His loving kindness and learn to also put Him first. Song of Solomon continues as the King says in verse 2, "As a lily among brambles, so is my love among the young women." You are a lily in all its splendor, so beautiful that all around you look like mere thorns! When you give place for this in your heart, you will see His provision for your heart, the fruit that He supplies, is more than anyone else in the world can provide! He is pleased to lavish you with value and love so that your eyes will be open to receive and feel His full acceptance of you as a reality in your life. The name "Sharon" in Song of Solomon 2:1 comes from a root that means pleasing. Beloved, among the many that are pleasing, you stand out with radiant beauty and emit an intoxicating fragrance to the King! You are a lily that clearly shines out of a valley of darkness. This is how your King sees you. You honor Him when you receive that revelation.

**ACTIVATION:**

Jesus, plant that seed of acceptance and immeasurable worth you see in me. Water it constantly, Jesus, until it grows deep roots in my heart and bears abundant fruit to honor you and lift up others.

*"As an apple tree among the trees of the forest, so is my beloved among the young men. With great delight I sat in his shadow, and his fruit was sweet to my taste." Song of Solomon 2:3*

Oh, beloved, what tree do you eat from? In this world, there are many lovers who vie for your affections. There is a forest all around you grasping for your gaze. There is only one, however, who is truly fruitful. You can stockpile all the world's goods, but your eyes will see nothing but lack and your heart will feel the drought. You may think that having more acceptance, status, power, or material goods will rescue your hungry soul; and for moments there may be a respite until lack knocks again creating a never-ending cycle of strife in the world.

When Jesus released me into full-time ministry, the leap was so far, especially financially, that I could not reach the other side; He would have to make up the difference. If He brought me to it, He was going to have to supply. Several months in, donations were coming in from grateful people to whom I ministered, but I also had to take up food delivery part-time to cover the difference. Do not despise humble beginnings because the Lord, again, provided so much more than some extra cash in that endeavor. He molded me with humility and provided opportunities for prayer and prophetic words over people in my community. Yet, I began to hunger for a bigger financial breakthrough. That week, I heard a sermon on sowing finances.

Although I believe God's dividends pay so much more than worldly capital, I knew there was truth in the principle of sowing, so I began to inquire of the Lord if I should sow in some way. I had a small savings account that I was protecting to cover upcoming income tax, and I didn't know how much of it I could spare. Any amount, really, would be a step of faith. He immediately gave me an amount and a local charity. Several mornings later, still wanting clarity and confirmation, I heard an amount double what I originally heard! Later that week, I conferred with a friend to listen to the Lord on my behalf. She heard a number almost double the larger amount! Contrary to worldly reasoning, my heart seemed to get excited at this. The amount was roughly 25% of all the cash in my possession. I know many others have given bigger percentages, but this stretched me. I waited until the weekend to be sure that the amount I heard stayed in my heart, and the next week I made the donation. When I pushed the last button to send the funds, it was as if I had pushed the peace button of heaven. I could have outright laughed with joy! I had tasted Jesus's fruit of obedience, and I received the joy that He had set before me. He had taken my focus from what I had in the natural realm and placed it on the riches I have in Him.

With great delight, the Shulamite sat in His shadow. Psalm 91:1-2 says, "He who dwells in the shelter of the Most High will abide in the shadow of the Almighty. I will say to the Lord, 'My refuge and my fortress, my God, in whom I trust.'" Certainly, this is a place we can run in panic and agony, but, beloved, Jesus paid for us to rest there in peace and delight. His shadow is not a storm shelter, cramped and barely supplied. It is a palace overflowing with His goodness, as we will see as He leads us into His banquet in the next verse of this song above all songs. But do not skip ahead too soon. To taste of the Lord is to taste goodness and satisfaction. *"Oh, taste and see that the Lord is good! Blessed is the man who takes refuge in him!" (Psalm 34:8).*

David penned this Psalm reflecting on his experience we read in 1 Samuel 21:10-15. David, running from Saul, entered an enemy kingdom for refuge. Feeling afraid, because they knew his successful battle history, he made himself appear insane. The king then sent him away.

Just before David suggests to the reader to taste the Lord's goodness; he writes, *"I sought the Lord, and he answered me and delivered me from all my fears. Those who look to him are radiant, and their faces shall never be ashamed" (Psalm 34:4-5).*

Do not look to the trees of working harder, looking prettier, or proving your worth. Look to the One, beloved, who truly nourishes you in every way. When you do, His radiance will shine upon you, and you will never be ashamed. The world may condemn you for being generous when it appears you are in lack, but the Lord will fill you to overflowing. Psalm 34:9 says, "Oh, fear the Lord, you his saints, for those who fear him have no lack!"

**ACTIVATION:**

Jesus, highlight the places I feel lack. I declare your lordship over those places. Is there any action, by faith, you would like for me to take so I can make space for you to heal my heart and mind, and so I can be lifted up above the cares of this world?

---

*"He brought me to the banqueting house, and his banner over me was love." Song of Solomon 2:4*

Indeed when we taste of the Lord, we will experience His goodness. As we ask, and even beg for more, we enter a place that Jesus calls "poor in spirit" (Matthew 5:3), which literally means to be a beggar for His Spirit. Jesus tells us that He will give His kingdom to these. In other words, this is a prayer to which His answer is always yes. This is echoed in Luke 11:13, "how much more will the heavenly Father give the Holy Spirit to those who ask him!"

I awoke one night, hearing the word, "Escondito." I had no idea what it meant, but I heard it so clear that I asked the Lord to help me remember it. After falling back asleep, I woke again with the word "En cantina." I heard it as all one word, and, again, I didn't understand. When I finally awoke for my morning quiet time with Jesus, I knew it was from Him because I could clearly remember the unknown terms. After some online searching and consulting my son who took Spanish in school, I discovered it was "Escondito en cantina" or hidden in the house of wine or in the bar. I asked Jesus why He had brought this to me. I saw a vision of Jesus as a bartender. The wall was stacked with bottles of every kind. There were shot glasses as well as a large wine bottle on the bar in front of Him. Each glass was labeled, and one was labeled "joy". "I have everything you need," He said. "There's no pain I can't ease; no trouble I can't comfort." Beloved, don't allow religion to offend you at this vision.

After all, Jesus used pigs to offend the religious Jews. The son who wasted his inheritance in Jesus's parable was reduced to working at a pig farm, the most repulsive place for a Jewish person.

Banqueting connotes lavish provision. If we attend a banquet, we think of a plethora of food, rich decor, and formal dress. Oh, how Jesus will provide the riches for your heart! Give Him your hurt, and your lack of understanding of why circumstances have occurred. Time and again I have seen visions of Him weeping over people in their traumatic memories and crying out that He never wanted this for them. "The Lord is near to the brokenhearted and saves the crushed in spirit" *(Psalm 34:18*). "Cast your burden on the Lord, and he will sustain you; he will never permit the righteous to be moved" *(Psalm 55:22).* When we see Jesus's heart for our circumstances, we have an opportunity to allow our hearts to be touched by His compassion and to see that He actually carries our burdens and pain. This releases our hold on the pain and allows Him to carry it.

After forgiving my grandfather, Jesus prepared my heart for greater depths of love and forgiveness that I didn't know were possible. In my morning quiet time, I had a vision come upon me, one I had not even known to seek on my own. I saw myself as very young, not even old enough to walk. I was in a pink jumper, pulling myself up on a wooden coffee table we had in my childhood apartment. My dad was laying on our bright blue couch. I could see Jesus sitting cross-legged on the floor. Then the vision switched to a man sitting in a pure white background with his elbows on his knees and his face downward. As I wondered who he was, he looked up. It was my grandfather, and tears were streaming down his face. "I'm sorry," he said, "I am so, so sorry." I began to cry a hard cry, and I called out, "I forgive you! I forgive you!"

Then the vision went back to me as a little baby. I crawled into Jesus's lap, pulled on His beard, and hugged Him. I now knew the other vision was in heaven. I saw the Father come to my grandfather, take him by the hand, and wrap His arms around my grandfather's shoulders as they walked away from me.

My grandfather went by the nickname Cricket, and as they walked away the Father said, "Your name is no longer Cricket. Now, you will be called Butterfly." I can only guess the meaning of this new name, which may have signaled new life or change, but I do know that tears of joy streamed down my face.

The wooden coffee table we had in our apartment was in the shape of the sun with slats of wood projecting outward and an opening in the middle with a metal decorative lid. The back story was that when my parents brought that table home from Mexico, they found it infested with roaches. In my vision, a hand sprayed the inside of that table, cleaned it out, and replaced the lid. Jesus had cleaned something out deep within me.

Switching again, I saw my grandfather kneeling before God's throne, his face to the floor and arms stretched outward. The Father came down from His throne, picked up my grandfather, and hugged him so tight that his feet came off the ground. With tears of joy flowing freely, I cried, "Bless him, Father! Bless him, Father!" At the apartment, Jesus stood my young self upon that clean coffee table, and the table turned into a large rock, The Rock. The One who is a firm foundation, restored my childhood and repaired years of damage the enemy created through causing hurt and attacking my identity.

Jesus walked me into deep levels of forgiveness I didn't know were possible. Now, I can't wait to see my grandfather in heaven. He gave his life to Jesus that day that I saw him sitting with the preacher in the kitchen. Jesus took the broken, the sinner, and made him a new creation, much like a butterfly. There's nothing we can do that Jesus's sacrifice is not rich enough to cover. My grandfather and I will have the relationship in heaven that was God's intention for us on the earth, and Jesus will restore, and already has restored, what the enemy had stolen. That, beloved, is His banquet. His banner over you is love. He celebrates you and gives you the reality of His victory in your heart and peace in your mind. The ultimate vengeance on the enemy is when both victim and perpetrator repent and surrender to Jesus, leaving the enemy fruitless in his attack.

**Activation:**

Jesus, help me surrender those who have hurt me to You so that you can vindicate me against the enemy in a way that heals the brokenhearted and invites new freedom of life in Your fullness.

*"Sustain me with raisins; refresh me with apples, for I am sick with love." Song of Solomon 2:5*

The original word for raisins means to be pressed together and the word apples means to inflate. Think of the exhale and inhale of breath. Sustain me with Your breath, Jesus, the breath that calls creation to life and creates galaxies of unimaginable riches we have yet to discover in the universe. I have fallen so in love with You that my soul constantly hungers for more of You. I yearn to feel Your closeness, not just know You are with me in my mind but to feel it in my soul. Touch my head and surround my heart *(Song of Solomon 2:6)* that there might be no part of me unaware of You, Immanuel, the God that is with me.

**ACTIVATION:**

Sit still, beloved, and allow his love to melt into your heart. Do not rush this moment. Sustain me with Your breath, Jesus. I am lovesick for You.

*"The voice of my beloved! Behold he comes, leaping over the mountains, bounding over the hills. My beloved is like a gazelle or a young stag. Behold, there he stands behind our wall, gazing through the windows, looking through the lattice. My beloved speaks and says to me, 'Arise, my love, my beautiful one, and come away,'" Song of Solomon 2:8-10*

How He runs toward you, beloved! The mountains of self-protection and the hills of misguided religion are but a track He bounds over to get to your heart. Yet, He is a gentleman. He will not tear down walls you don't invite Him through. He will remain on the other side of the window. He will lovingly gaze at you through the lattice, with His compassionate eyes calling you to the freedom He has paid for you. Arise, He says, to experience the garden in which you were created to walk alongside Him. Verses 10 through 13 describe a beautiful spring season with flowers, figs, and turtle doves. Adam and Eve used fig leaves to hide their bodies full of shame; let's tear off the fig leaves from our hearts. The enemy attacks what the Lord calls good in you, causing you to hide and feel condemned.

In the midst of my rejection as a senior in high school, I became pregnant by a boy who had shown interest in me. A teen girl, full of rejection, is an easy target for the enemy, especially when you couple that with a teen boy carrying his own hidden hurt. Through many tears, regrets, and confusion, I had an abortion. Only about a year later, I became pregnant again by that same boy. Feeling the rejection and lack of support again, I, unfortunately, made the same choice. My heart was becoming numb to sin because the sin was less painful than the rejection. Do not forget, though, beloved, that our battles are not with flesh and blood *(Ephesians 6:12)*. We have a very real enemy who wreaks havoc in the hearts of every human on some level. He is the author of evil and engages in warfare constantly against the image-bearers of God, believers and unbelievers alike. Though others' actions may have contributed to the end result, our vision of truth was skewed by the enemy's work in our own hearts and minds.

Decades later, I began my intentional inner-healing journey. I sat across from a loving man who exuded the Father's tenderness and care. He had me prayerfully read Shadow Boxing by Dr. Henry Malone, and discussed with me the issues the Lord brought up with each chapter. One day as I sat and listened to him, a voice began screaming in my mind. I remember him asking if he could move on to the next topic, but I couldn't understand anything he said. I finally apologized and told him about the loud voice of accusation I couldn't escape internally. I began to sob as I heard accusations from the enemy condemning me for the abortions. In response, this man gently hugged me with the Father's arms. He never asked me what the accuser was saying; he just held me and encouraged me to cry it all out. Later, I had a vision of Jesus washing my feet that seemed so real. Isn't that like our Beloved to wash away the dirt of the world so that we may walk as spotless ones before Him?

**ACTIVATION:**

Ask Jesus what accusations He would love to cleanse you of today. Give Him permission.

---

*"Oh my dove, in the clefts of the rock, in the crannies of the cliff, let me see your face, let me hear your voice, for your voice is sweet, and your face is lovely." Song of Solomon 2:14*

Unlike Moses, we who believe are under the New Covenant and are no longer sinners who must hide in the rock to see the face of our Savior. The body and blood of Jesus has fully paid for us to come before God. Our sinful nature is gone, so we may stand confidently as sons and daughters. The Bridegroom wants to see our face! We don't have to be the veiled bride in Song of Solomon 1 or the veiled leader of Exodus 34. His glory now shines freely on us and even in us! The enemy would love for us to remain behind the window and behind the lattice, holding onto our shame and the enemy's accusation. The enemy loves darkness, secrets, and hiding; but the Word says, *"Therefore, confess your sins to one another and pray for one another, that you may be healed. The prayer of a righteous person has great power as it is working"—James 5:16.*

He is faithful to partner with your search for true freedom by catching the little foxes that spoil the vineyards (Song of Solomon 2:15).

**ACTIVATION:**

Share your story with a trustworthy friend, inviting Jesus into the shame and condemnation. This is the great power to receive healing and shut down the voices trying to deceive you out of your true identity as a son or daughter of the King!

---

*"My beloved is mine, and I am his; he grazes among the lilies. Until the day breathes and the shadows flee, turn, my beloved, be like a gazelle or a young stag on cleft mountains."*
*Song of Solomon 2:16-17*

He is jealous for our hearts, beloved. This is how we surrender more of ourselves to Him and put ourselves more and more into the safe fortress of His love: we give Him all the ugly places in our hearts so He can make them beautiful. He is not looking for us to impress Him; He is looking for us to lay bare before Him. This way, He can clothe us in His splendor. "Consider the lilies how they grow; they toil not, they spin not; and yet I say unto you, that Solomon in all his glory was not arrayed like one of these" *(Luke 12:27)*. When we keep the religious mask in place—hiding our true selves, story, and testimony from the world—we are like a sheep going off to care for itself. But, oh, our Shepherd is a persistent pursuer of our hearts. We, in our journey with Him, will always be the one He goes after. Whether we are hurting or joyful, He is the pursuer of our attention and adoration. He knows that when we gaze upon Him, we have all we need in His presence. My ESV footnote says that grazing in the lilies can also mean pasture a flock. I pray we can receive His lavish joy and celebration when we, His sheep and prodigals, are found. May we never identify with the resentful older brother of the prodigal son, who had no need of the Shepherd or His grace. May we constantly abide with the One who is the pursuer of our heart! You are not only a beautiful lily in the darkest valley, but you are the sheep He longs to lavish with His tender care. He is the gazelle or stag that climbs over the mountains of your heart; He will remain there until the shadows flee and you feel His breath of life in your soul.

During my journey, I participated in a Bible study with two friends that focused on healing the hearts of women who had suffered abortions. In the study, one of our activities was to ask the Lord to see our aborted children and ask Him information about them, including their names. When I asked, I saw a tanned skin girl, around 5 years old, with curly black hair and a purple shirt. She was in the arms of Jesus and nuzzling noses with Him. I also saw a little boy, around age 3, playfully frolicking around; he was carefree and joyful. He too had tanned skin and curly black hair, as well as a blue button-down that barely covered his little round belly. These children were not forgotten or erased. As stated in Isaiah 49:15, *"Can a woman forget her nursing child, that she should have no compassion on the son of her womb? Even these may forget, yet I will not forget you."*

I may have been too wounded to make good choices about my pregnancies, but God, in His faithfulness, cared for them and healed the missing piece of my broken heart. I acknowledge that many women make the brave choice to keep their children even in their hurt and woundedness. I will always champion them. I also celebrate a Savior who takes the ashes of our brokenness and exchanges them for beauty.

Since then, I have been blessed to see several family members and close friends in visions like this one. I have even seen pets. These glimpses into heaven bring me peace beyond comprehension and ease my heart from the sting of their passing. For this reason, I can grieve as someone with much hope!

**ACTIVATION:**

Beloved, play the song "Your Love is Strong" by Cory Asbury. Let the Lord sing over you and let the words water seeds of love He has placed in your heart. May their roots grow deep and your fruit be abundant.

*"On my bed by night I sought him whom my soul loves; I sought him, but found him not. I will rise now and go about the city, in the streets and in the squares; I will see him whom my soul loves. I sought him, but found him not. The watchmen found me as they went about in the city. 'Have you seen him whom my soul loves?' Scarcely had I passed them when I found him whom my soul loves. I held him, and would not let him go until I had brought him into my mother's house, and into the chamber of her who conceived me." Song of Solomon 3:1-4*

As a young mom with small children, I used to wake up about 15 minutes before I had to wake up my children, so I could sip my coffee and watch the news before the rush of the day. After a while, I got tired of the depressing news stories that used to circulate for a week before moving on to more depressing news. Instead, I decided to spend that time with Jesus. I made a choice to read a devotional and write a short journal entry, which led to increasing amounts of devotional time and journal writing in the mornings that followed. I began to ponder scripture on my own and ask questions that hadn't been answered for me in church. When I asked friends about these questions, their answers just led to more questions. Questions to my pastors were, at times, skipped over all together. My spiritual father once told me that "Scripture raises questions that only relationship can answer." I certainly found that to be true. I only found these answers as I slowly pondered them with Jesus in the mornings.

Soon, I began to experience sensations in my body I could not explain. The first was a warm chill, a tingling in my body usually from the back of my head and down my spine when I would pray. I would also feel pressure on my chest that was not uncomfortable but captured my attention. Then, during devotionals at our preschool staff meeting, I began experiencing bouts of unexplained shaking when I felt compelled to say something the Lord wanted me to add to the discussions. During one of these experiences, I excused myself to the prayer room, and I cried to God that I knew these manifestations were of Him but I had no idea what I was to do with them.

I also began full-on crying at even simple prayer requests. I first experienced this at a prayer meeting where we could pick up a few cards with prayer requests and then again at a preschool conference where the speaker was talking about prayer requests her students had submitted to her. I cried so hard I knew it would disrupt, but I just could not hold it in. The tears were too much to stay in the rooms, so I would leave and seek the Lord. As I talked to a friend about these experiences, she suggested I attend a local Bible college that was better known for charismatic freedom than direct theology. I dismissed it at first, but I took one small step at a time, filled out the application, and found myself there. I was much older than most students and attended part-time hoping to taste the world of the supernatural of God. He was busting out of the box I had Him in, and I had no comprehension of it.

This, beloved, is what it can look like to get past the watchmen. Watchmen, most times, mean well. If we are leaders in the kingdom in any capacity, I see us as watchmen. Watchmen help others to find Jesus, but they themselves must know what He looks like. If we forever stay by the watchmen, then we are just receiving someone else's chewed revelation and have no fresh bread of our own. In chapter 1, the king encourages the Shulamite to pasture her goats beside the shepherds' tents, but we cannot stay there. Every time we hear a sermon, read a book about Him, or speak to someone about Him, the question from our heart should be, "Have you seen Him?" If they have, then we will know Him when we see Him. Beloved, if others around you can't help you know Him, you must move past them to find Him on your own. In fact, every Shulamite who continues in the love affair with Jesus must get to this place.

Knowing Him has no end. There will be times you may be misunderstood. Many times this is the enemy thwarting your search to find the One whom your soul loves. Just as you pass them, you will find Him! I saw many at that Bible college experiencing what I had experienced, and I knew the Lord had sent me there. I cried at finding answers and guidance in what my heart had been experiencing and seeking.

Chapel was freeing at this college. Some stood with their arms stretched up, some laid face down on the floor, and others cried at His presence. One morning, I stood with my arms high. I felt an urge to kneel, but, honestly, I was still in the process of learning to surrender and experience the freedom of worship. I began to hear a conversation in the spirit between Satan and Jesus. Satan said, "She won't do it." Jesus said, "Yes, she will. She's mine." I knew I had to kneel. When I fell to my knees, tears streaming, I saw Jesus wrap me in a white robe. I heard Him say, "Just like Jonathan gave David." I remembered Jonathan gave David some armor or weapons, and I planned to look up the details later. The experience was so real that I felt I still wore the robe after chapel ended. Later that afternoon, I remembered the words of Jesus and looked up the story. Scripture states, *"The soul of Jonathan was knit to the soul of David, and Jonathan loved him as his own soul...Then Jonathan made a covenant with David because he loved him as his own soul. And Jonathan stripped himself of the robe that was on him and gave it to David, and his armor, and even his sword and his bow and his belt" 1 Sam 18:1, 3-4.*

When I read the word robe in scripture, my eyes swelled again with tears, and I pondered over and over "because he loved him as his own soul". Jesus loves us as He loves Himself. He never commands us to do anything He hasn't already accomplished. More than that, He made a way to wrap us in His robe of righteousness *(Isaiah 61:10)*, and Ephesians 6 explains all the armor of God He has provided. Beloved, did you know that Jesus loves you as He loves Himself? In fact, He laid His life down for you, putting you before Himself. We get revelations of truth in that love if we seek it for ourselves. When you find Him, don't let go! Bring Jesus into your most intimate places. Allow Him to have your dignity, not only in worship but in obedience. You'll find that you will have dignity, but it won't be an image you are trying to protect: it will be a more glorious image He has planned for you.

Song of Solomon 3:4 echoes Genesis 24:67, "Then Isaac brought her into the tent of Sarah his mother and took Rebekah, and she became his wife, and he loved her." The

Shulamite desires to make Him her own. We cannot hang on to a Christian heritage; we must seek a Christ experience. We cannot simply inherit the beliefs of our parents and grandparents and call ourselves Christian as if it were a geographical location or part of our ancestry. In a Jewish wedding after the ceremony, the bride and groom get a few minutes to themselves in a private room, a tradition called Yichud. They get away from the rush of the festivities and are escorted by their families to this room where they often exchange gifts and soak in the moment together. Beloved, have you had your very own wedding with Jesus? Do you steal away moments to soak in Him, allowing the exchange of gifts as you praise Him and He pours eternal riches from heaven upon you?

**ACTIVATION:**

Sit still. Tell Him His value to you. Allow His love to flow back into your heart and to pour in the truth of who you are to Him.

*"What is that coming up from the wilderness like columns of smoke, perfumed with myrrh and frankincense, with all the fragrant powders of a merchant? Behold, it is the litter of Solomon! Around it are sixty mighty men, some of the mighty men of Israel, all of them wearing swords and expert in war, each with his sword at his thigh, against terror by night."*
*Song of Solomon 3:6-8*

These columns of smoke remind us of the cloud by day and fire by night in the Israelites' wilderness of Exodus 13. Imagine being in a hot dry desert only to see a parade of the king coming through. What a glorious sign of civilization to a weary soul. Scripture states, "When Pharoah let the people go, God did not lead them by way of the land of the Philistines, although that was near. For God said, 'Lest the people change their minds when they see war and return to Egypt.' But God led the people around by way of the wilderness toward the Red Sea. And the people of Israel went up out of the land of Egypt equipped for battle" *(Exodus 13:17-18)*. If God led the Israelites around the long way through the wilderness to keep them from going back to Egypt, how many times does He take us the long way around so we will leave the comfortable place of bondage to bring us into a journey of trusting Him? The good news is

He is with us in the wilderness, guiding us, providing for us, and, most importantly, cultivating relationship and trust with us. Our loving King is sitting on a sedan chair ("litter") called a mercy seat, traveling in our wilderness with all the riches we need for our thirsty souls. His people, the Israelites, have carried this inheritance for us for thousands of years. They have endured the wrath of persecution because of this glorious truth, and now we are partakers of this divine plan to put us in communion with Creator God, the satisfier of our hearts.

Beloved, it doesn't matter the path you have taken to find the King: He beckons your heart to come. Aren't we glad He does not despise being the God of last resort? I had tried every pleasure of the world before I finally succumbed to His beckoning, His true life, and His freedom. He once gave me a vision of Himself following me everywhere I went with a water jug ready to relieve me of my spiritual thirst at any moment. He followed me to every bar, stood by, and cried at every choice that wedged my heart away from Him; He waited patiently knowing one day I would be fully His. See Him coming out of the wilderness in all of His glory, just for you, beloved. He meets you where you are, anywhere you are. He gave it all just at the chance that you might say yes. Say yes (maybe again) today.

**ACTIVATION:**

Tell Him how you feel about Him. He loves to hear it. Then wait. You will hear something beautiful in return.

---

*"King Solomon made himself a carriage from the wood of Lebanon. He made its posts of silver, its back of gold, its seat of purple; its interior was inlaid with love by the daughters of Jerusalem. Go out, O daughters of Zion, and look upon King Solomon, with the crown with which his mother crowned him on the day of his wedding, on the day of the gladness of his heart."*
*Song of Solomon 3:9-11*

How this carriage echoes the Ark of the Covenant that was carried on the shoulders of the Israelites and is now the easy yoke that is carried on the shoulders of men who call upon Him. Jeremiah 3:16 prophesies we will no longer remember the Ark, but all nations will gather to the presence of the Lord in Jerusalem: "And when you have multiplied and been fruitful in the land, in those days, declares the Lord, they shall no more say, 'The ark of the covenant of the Lord.'" Jeremiah 3:16 is the prophetic word preceding John 3:16. The Father would send His Son to take our eyes off of the ark and put them on

His very own Son. This carriage is the place created for us by the sacrifice of Jesus.

This carriage is the theme of Psalm 91:1-2; it's a secret place, a shadow, a refuge, and a fortress. In this protective relationship with Jesus, we find all we will ever need. Consider the contents of the ark, the stone tablets, the budding rod of Aaron, and the manna. The commandments of the Lord are our loving instruction from a good Father teaching us how to avoid playing in the street of enemy activity and to stay in the safety of His playground of life.

The budding rod is the authority given to us through the victory of King Jesus to stand as kings and priests in the earth. The manna is a constant physical, emotional, and spiritual provision for us as children of the Most High God. In this carriage of the King, we find everything we need, beloved: protection, authority, and provision.

Inside this carriage of Solomon, we find silver, gold, and purple. The silver and gold remind us of the first chapter where the King lavishes His bride with compliments, wooing her away from the darkness she sees upon herself. Song of Solomon 1:11 ends the serenade, "We will make you ornaments of gold, studded with silver." Beloved, this carriage is inlaid with love.

Here, He will remind you who you are over and over. He invites you to see yourself as royalty, and His great love delights in this truth. We, who are in Him, are no longer sinners. The old cliche, "Just a sinner saved by grace," is a trap by the enemy, and the hold of its teeth keeps believers trapped under a lie and away from the fullness of His freedom. "We know that our old self was crucified with him in order that the body of sin might be brought to nothing so that we would no longer be enslaved to sin" *(Romans 6:6)*. God is not afraid to give you too much beauty for your ashes. He is confident in who He is and never fears inflating a heart that is hungry for Him and bows in thankfulness before Him.

When I was still processing my memories of abuse, I had a memory from my grandfather's house that carried a sting. I invited Jesus into that ugly, shameful memory. I was so young and sought attention from adults around me. When I became a little older and realized the dysfunction of my grandfather's attention, the enemy began spewing shame all over me for freely receiving that attention when I was too young to understand. Jesus entered that memory. He wrapped me in a white robe or blanket and carried me out of the house. On the country road beyond the front yard, a procession of a king came. I recognized the King coming in my wilderness, and I ran toward the carriage. As I ran, my clothing began to disintegrate and turn into a beautiful bridal gown. The carriage stopped for me, and I entered. Oh, the Father was there! I wrapped my arms around His welcoming neck, and He took me away. The Father's compassion stole me away from the enemy's entrapment.

Isn't that like our enemy? He will attack you and then find a way to shame you for his attack. Seek the Lord's carriage. The interior of His carriage is inlaid with love *(Song of Sol. 3:10)*. This is the wedding for which He gave everything so that you might agree to be His bride; it is the day of the gladness of His heart *(Song of Sol. 3:11)*.

**ACTIVATION:**

Run to the carriage, beloved. Let Jesus remove you from the shame of your past and release you into His Father's love and acceptance. He will lavish you with jewels of silver and gold in His love and remind you who you are.

*"Behold, you are beautiful, my love, behold, you are beautiful! Your eyes are doves behind your veil." Song of Solomon 4:1*

Do you know the King thinks you are beautiful? If you have ever experienced love, you know that whether it's a new boyfriend or girlfriend or a new baby, even their flaws find space in your heart for praise. We think quirks are cute as we easily overlook imperfections, gazing into their eyes and pondering the love in our hearts. I asked Jesus one morning, "Jesus, give me a vision of how you see me." I saw a picture of a woman I believed to be Eve, covered in natural vines and holding a confident posture. My first thought was, "Oh no! The lady that disobeyed and ate the fruit." Jesus quickly captured that thought and responded, "That's not how I see her.

Eve walked with me in the cool of the day." I could feel the pleasure in His heart of their unhindered relationship, and how He even delighted in her after the fall, making her the first mother of all His creation. He chose not to remember her mistakes. He chose to remember her. He does the same with you. He looks into your eyes and sees doves of peace and rest. As you look at Him, He sees the reflection of Himself in your eyes. Even when you are weak and look away, He woos you back into His gaze and forgets that you ever looked away. We don't repent for our poor choices because we have offended God; we repent because of His generous mercy and quick forgiveness.

We are not defined by the times we forgot who we are, beloved; we are defined by His words of love. He says your lips are like scarlet *(Song of Sol. 4:3)*. When you utter your praise and adoration for Him, He revels in your devotion. He is reminded of Rahab's scarlet rope: a symbol of her faithfulness to God's people and His own streams of blood that flowed down His body in a beautiful sacrifice for us, His bride. Your attention is the sacrifice of praise you are able to give today. He doesn't look at your wavering. He looks at your intention; He looks at the true desire of your heart. Do you say, "But I don't know if my desire is purely for Him!" Do not worry, beloved. Hand even this to Him who returns no condemnation or shame. He will replace dry places with fountains of living water.

Vulnerability and honesty with Him prepare the soil in your heart and allow Him to plant His goodness. When I laid the shame of my past choices desperately at His feet, He showed me how I had been grasping for life for all those years. I had walked into sin, deeper and deeper, and my heart had become more and more numb, desensitized to the alarms of impending danger in my soul. Jesus said to me, "You became naked and unashamed before man, but you were made to have a heart naked and unashamed before Me." Give Jesus your shame.

**ACTIVATION:**

Ask Him to forgive your poor life choices, so that He has permission to enter those places in your heart and replace them with His acceptance and grace.

---

*"You are altogether beautiful, my love; there is no flaw in you. Come with me from Lebanon, my bride; come with me from Lebanon. Depart from the peak of Amana, from the peak of Senir and Hermon, from the dens of lions, from the mountains of leopards." Song of Solomon 4:7-8*

There is no flaw in you. Most would think that is quite a pompous statement without any of the humility we are called to as Christians. This is not a self-proclaimed statement but one that is made by a King whose blood has cleansed all. Paul says this in 2 Corinthians,

*"From now on, therefore, we regard no one according to the flesh. Even though we once regarded Christ according to the flesh, we regard him thus no longer. Therefore, if anyone is in Christ, he is a new creation. The old has passed away; behold, the new has come." 2 Corinthians 5:16-17*

And he says again in Romans 6, *"just as Christ was raised from the dead by the glory of the Father, we too might walk in newness of life...We know that our old self was crucified with him in order that the body of sin might be brought to nothing, so that we may no longer be enslaved to sin. For one who has died has been set free of sin... you also must consider yourselves dead to sin and alive to God in Christ Jesus" (Romans 6:4, 6, 11).*

You are not a sinner! When you said yes to Jesus, your old spirit died and your new spirit resurrected with His spirit, merging as one to make you flawless. Then why do those who are reborn still sin? They do not know who they are. My spiritual father likes to ask the question, "Did Eve need a sin nature to sin in the garden?" The enemy came with deception and questioned her identity and the goodness of God, suggesting He was holding back goodness from her. She was dis-EVE-ed, or convinced out of her true identity! She was convinced that she was not as wholly loved as she actually was by God. When we are reborn and make poor choices, we are not living out of our true nature but out of an old nature that's already dead. You are altogether beautiful! Turn from the enemy's lions and leopards that steal your identity.

I once lived heavily in people-pleasing. This was a perversion of my love for serving others that, without me consciously realizing it, added an expectation for others to fill my heart with value in return. Eventually, I found myself weary of giving without recognition, promotion, or return in some way. Additionally, I compared myself to others in an attempt to receive more value and judged others who didn't seem to measure up. As I began receiving freedom, I realized that I had trouble shaking comparison and judgment. Also, my heart felt crushed whenever I did not receive overt appreciation for my efforts. However, as I sat, morning after morning, and allowed Jesus to remind me who I was, I began to give up serving where I wasn't called, even in positions of notoriety in the church. These positions were nothing compared to the infilling I was receiving from the One who is life. I began to follow His lead on the new positions He planned for me. I was delivered of the demonic spirits of people-pleasing, comparison, and judgment. I became free to learn new ways of thinking about myself and others. In partnership with Jesus, I began to champion others in their gifts and accomplishments. I laid down dead works in my own strength for works in partnership with Jesus that were an overflow of love. I laid down deception for truth. My wounded soul had to catch up to my spirit that was made perfect with Jesus.

**Activation:**

Repeat, beloved, "I am not a sinner. I am dead to sin." He sees you as flawless and beautiful. He is a perfectly yoked Bridegroom to His bride, even now when you may not feel it.

---

*"You have captivated my heart, my sister, my bride; you have captivated my heart with one glance of your eyes, with one jewel of your necklace. How beautiful is your love, my sister, my bride! How much better is your love than wine, and the fragrance of your oils than any spice!" Song of Solomon 4:9-10*

Captivated (Strongs H3823) in this verse means to encourage. You encourage the King! He calls you sister (or brother) because we are "predestined to be conformed to the image of his Son, in order that He might be the firstborn among many brothers" *(Romans 8:29)*. No one ever achieves a goal by focusing on where they used to be. We envision our goal and declare it over ourselves until we reach our goal of Christ-likeness. When we continue to walk toward our goal of purity in Him, Jesus's heart is encouraged by us and captivated by our surrender to Him. Just a glance of your eyes toward His, looking toward your goal, your prize, your love, creates delight in Him. You are your Father's favorite.

Sometimes, He graciously allows me to feel some of His delight and love for others. When this happens, I feel as though I know them, even though they are strangers, and I will weep with joy over them. They appear as the most beautiful people, no matter their outward appearance. They seem like the kindest people I've ever met, no matter their small gestures at that moment. Their smiles brighten my heart. The Father told me that is how He feels as He looks at each of His children, and He is able to look at each one of us in unison. When I tell others that I feel the Father's love over them and they see my weeping eyes, His Spirit seems to touch theirs as they reach out for hugs and exclaim gratefulness. We all need to know that we captivate His heart, our love is precious to Him, and our lives are a pleasing aroma to Him.

**ACTIVATION:**

Jesus, I invite You to fill me with Your love and acceptance right now. Fill me so full that I tangibly feel it within and on my body. Now, wait on Him, beloved.

*"Your lips drip nectar, my bride; honey and milk are under your tongue; the fragrance of your garments is like the fragrance of Lebanon. A garden locked is my sister, my bride, a spring locked, a fountain sealed." Song of Solomon 4:11-12*

Isn't that like Jesus? He has just completed a beautiful soliloquy over His bride, gushing about her beauty, and then He tells her that her lips and mouth are sweet like nectar and honey. What a gracious Bridegroom who calls out His bride into who she is! He is wooing her into praise of Him, as we will see in the next chapter. He knows the secret to her confidence and beauty: when she receives what He has for her, she can freely worship and venture into greater depths with Him.

*We are made alive together with Christ; we are raised up with Him, and He has "seated us with him in heavenly places in Christ Jesus so that in the coming ages he might show the immeasurable riches of his grace in kindness toward us in Christ Jesus" (Ephesians* 2:5-7).

The word ages (Strongs G165) can be interpreted from the original language as "evermore". We are seated in heavenly places with our King so that from now on He can fill us with His immeasurable riches. Our gracious King does not give us obscure sayings that leave us just short of understanding how to receive His goodness. Envision the heavenly places in your mind. I have described some of the heavenly places that I have seen, beloved. Jesus wants to fill you with His immeasurable riches, showing you the truth of your priceless worth to Him, for who can put a price on the Son of God's life that He gave for you? He wants to cultivate trust and relationship with you so that you know His character. Then, when you read His Word, the scriptures, from this place, His heart comes alive within its words.

As your heart fills with truth, your praise will flow to His heart because to know Him is to continue to love Him more. This is nectar and honey to Him. You become a garden and a spring bursting forth with life for Him to enjoy with you. On this earth, He had no place to rest His head, but beloved, He now has a place to rest in you. I once saw Jesus in a garden, laying on a hammock, with sunglasses and an umbrella drink. When I saw this, I giggled and cried at the same time, because I was excited to see that my heart was a comfortable place for Him.

These experiences, beloved, are the immeasurable riches that can never be stolen from you. No matter what life brings, there is security that the King of Kings has your heart and no man can steal it unless you allow it. You are a locked garden just for the King, a fountain sealed.

*"Let my beloved come to his garden, and eat its choicest fruits" Song of Solomon 4:16.*

**ACTIVATION:**

Jesus, I give you permission to meet with me in heavenly places. Will you meet me in the garden of my heart? I receive your riches in my heart so that my praise can also grow in love toward You.

*"I slept, but my heart was awake. A sound! My beloved is knocking. 'Open to me, my sister, my love, my dove, my perfect one, for my head is wet with dew, my locks with the drops of the night.' I had put off my garment; how could I put it on? I had bathed my feet; how could I soil them?"Song of Solomon 5:2-3*

God will leave you in your comfortable place for a time, but only for a time if you are to grow in greater depths with Him. In this comfortable place, we know more of His word. We get more set in our theology and may even find fellowship with like-minded people. It's a beautiful place, but King Jesus always has more for those who seek. Keep your heart awake to Him. He is faithful to knock, and your steps of faith will bring you to higher places. He will bring you opportunities to forfeit your worldly dignity for His heavenly dignity. He will bring you to a place where you may look like a fool to the world, but those who have traveled these roads with Him will spot your devotion to Him. This devotion is worth giving up the praise of the world. "The natural person does not accept the things of the Spirit of God, for they are folly to him, and he is not able to understand them because they are spiritually discerned" *(1 Corinthians 2:14)*. God is not primarily interested in man's acceptance of you; He is more interested in capturing the part of your heart that you render to man's acceptance. If your cleaned-up appearance is for the approval of others, He will invite you to surrender to the messy and unpredictable way of His love. He is not looking for a prim and proper bride but one that is sold out to Him in loving obedience.

I was at a home Bible church one Friday night. We sat in a tight circle in the living room as the host belted out beautiful praise. We sang along, some with eyes closed, and some with hands upturned or slightly raised. As we worshipped, I saw a vision of myself face down on the floor and felt He was asking me to physically bow at that moment. "I don't want to make something of myself," I replied. "Will you make something of Me?" He asked. Oh, beloved! My heart was convicted so gently. Who was my King in comparison to how others saw me? I dropped to my knees, face planted, and sobbed with outstretched arms the remainder of worship. Someone later, half-jokingly, asked if anyone needed prayer except me. I'm sure that was a humorous way to address the obvious display that had just transpired, but my joy was not removed. I was holding a treasure in my heart, a joy so deep that I shared with Jesus, that I felt no obligation to explain. Our joy is to obey, and the consequences of that obedience belong to the Lord.

**ACTIVATION:**

Jesus, I give you my comfort and dignity in exchange for more of You. I welcome Your nudges of encouragement to show radical displays of love to a King who showed a radical display of love for me on the cross.

---

*"I arose to open to my beloved, and my hands dripped with myrrh, my fingers with liquid myrrh, on the handles of the bolt. I opened to my beloved, but my beloved had turned and gone. My soul failed me when he spoke. I sought him, but found him not; I called him, but he gave no answer." Song of Solomon 5:5-6*

I certainly would have no understanding of this passage had I not experienced it myself. How could the kindness of Jesus allow for Him to leave when we reach for Him? I submit, beloved, that it is only our perception. He never leaves nor forsakes us *(Deuteronomy 31:6, Hebrews 13:5)*, and if the word seems to disagree with itself, then we have to have the Holy Spirit reveal the truth to our hearts.

I had been experiencing God in ways at the Bible college that I had never experienced elsewhere at that point. While there, I kept hearing about the Azusa Revival, and it drew my heart. One day, I watched a documentary about it, and, midway through the documentary, the narrator encouraged the viewer to pause the video and read Acts 2. At every line I read, my heart grew restless and my physical body followed. I was scheduled to take my son to a check-up appointment that morning, but I found myself too shaken and asked my husband to go instead. I wasn't shaken in a negative sense, but, at the same time, I had no understanding of what to do. Looking back, I would describe the feeling like this: before, I was like a vase filled with the water of Jesus, and, after, I was like a lake-size vessel filled with the same amount of water as the vase. It wasn't that Jesus had left; it was that I needed more of Him to fill me.

Desperation seemed to rush over me. Paul wrote to the Corinthian church, "You are not restricted by us, but you are restricted in your own affections. In return (I speak as to children) widen your hearts also" *(2 Corinthians 6:12-13).* I decided to go to my home church and seek their help. When I tried to explain my plight and feelings of desperation, one staff member began praying for Jesus to deliver me. I immediately knew this was incorrect and refused it.

When two more staff members came, I tried to explain my feelings, but they were lost in how to help me. In fact, some of their words were hurtful.

Without answers, I decided to drive to the Bible college 30 to 40 minutes away in hopes I'd find someone with answers. As I drove, I left a message for one of my teachers; however, once there, I found no one. I was alone and desperate to fill this new emptiness. Thankfully, my teacher called me back, and, upon sharing my dilemma, he laughed a laugh that brought me comfort. It was a laugh of recognition. "You have revival in your heart, Rhonda," he said. I really had little idea of what that meant but peace seemed to drip into my mind, and I welcomed this new feeling. Later as I sat with Jesus, talking to Him, worshiping and praising Him, that space began to fill within me, and I felt more loved than I ever had before.

**ACTIVATION:**

Tell Jesus you will make space in your heart for what He wants to do. Set the table of your heart for your Beloved. Allow Him to feast, to fill, or to empty as He pleases. Wait on Him.

*"The watchmen found me as they went about in the city; they beat me, they bruised me, they took away my veil, those watchmen of the walls." Song of Solomon 5:7*

As watchmen leaders of a flock of Jesus's beloveds, we must make room for Him to move in ways in which we are unfamiliar. Leaders' intentions are rarely evil, and the leaders I encountered were trying to help. As seekers of His face, our focus is to pass the watchmen, as described in chapter 3, and not allow leaders to abuse us or talk us out of our pursuit of the depths of God. Many leaders in the church experience much stress; and they often feel they have to appear perfect to their congregants, leaving them with no place to rest their true hearts.

Each Shulamite is on her own journey with King Jesus. Do not let anyone hinder yours, beloved. Instead, let the SOS of your heart cry out for the Song of Solomon heart of the King; seek nearness with your Beloved and tell him, "I am sick with love" *(Song of Solomon 5:8)*.

**ACTIVATION:**

My heart cries out for You. I ask for revival in my heart like a fire that burns so brightly and freely that it honors You and catches onto others around me.

---

*"My beloved is radiant and ruddy, distinguished among ten thousand." Song of Solomon 5:10*

Jesus is radiantly God and ruddy, which means reddish, as a man. He is God in that He is exalted and high. He is man in that He is Immanuel, God with us. He is not just a man who once walked the earth as we do, but He's closer, beloved. He has poured His riches into your heart; given you beauty for the ashes that once covered you in shame, wounds, and lies; and now you are free to feel the tangible love He has for you. His love has always been flowing to you, but now your heart can receive it deeply. His words of love spoken over you now give you the confidence to answer when others ask, "What is your beloved more than another beloved?" *(Song of Solomon 5:9)* Peter tells us to sanctify Christ as Lord in our hearts *(1 Peter 3:15)*. We do this by continuing to walk with Him, encounter Him, and renewing our minds with His word.

Just as a friend, we grow trust through relationship. The more we see His character, the more beautiful, loving, and trustworthy He looks. The closer we get, the more clearly we see Him. Then Peter tells us to always be prepared to offer an explanation to anyone who asks us to justify the hope that is in you *(1 Peter 3:15)*. We are only prepared to the degree we have experienced Him, and that's perfect! If we have experienced the freedom of initial salvation in our hearts, we have that testimony to share. If we have deep roads of love poured out, then we have that to share.

Here, the Shulamite gushes over her Bridegroom because no one else will do. "His head is the finest gold" *(Song of Solomon 5:11)* because He has nothing but perfect thoughts and plans for us. There is no impure or unrighteous intent for our lives within Him.

"His eyes are like doves beside streams of water" *(Song of Solomon 5:12)* because He longs to wash us. Just as He washed the feet of His disciples, including Judas who betrayed Him, He longs to cleanse us of the dirt of the world so we can walk in His freedom.

"His cheeks are like beds of spices…His lips are lilies" *(Song of Solomon 5:13)* because He displays all the fruits of the Spirit and makes His garden available to us. Like Boaz left sheaves behind for Ruth to glean *(Ruth 2:15)*, you will find favor in the eyes of

King Jesus, and He will always speak love and acceptance to you. Even His words of correction will drip with love and pull you into His goodness.

"His arms are rods of gold, set with jewels" (Song of Solomon 5:14) because He is able to protect His beloved. His arms are the shelter of the Most High, the shadow of the Almighty, our refuge, and our fortress (Psalm 91:1-2).

"His legs are alabaster columns, set on bases of gold" (Song of Solomon 5:15) because He has all authority. Think of the stout columns of a courthouse or city hall.

*"All authority in heaven and on earth has been given to Me" Matthew 28:18.*

Beloved, your King conquered every demonic force, even death, that He might rightfully walk in all authority, and now it is yours to wield with Him to fight the battles in your life, as well as for others. "His mouth is most sweet, and he is altogether desirable. This is my beloved and this is my friend" *(Song of Solomon 5:16)* because He is good and true. This is an echo of Song of Solomon 4:7, where the King calls His bride altogether beautiful with no flaw in her. She is learning to honor Him because of the honor He has mercifully and generously poured on her. Her heart is full of His love, and she calls Him friend.

I love that Psalm 139:14 says, *"I praise you, for I am fearfully and wonderfully made. Wonderful are your works; my soul knows it well."* The word fearfully is the same word yare (Strongs H3373), which means to be reverent, and is also used in Psalm 66:16, "Come and hear, all you who fear God...." God does not worship or fear us as His creation, but He sings over us *(Zephaniah 3:17)*. We love because He first loved us *(1 John 4:19)*, and He was in awe of us as His children in whom He delights. One does not honor a creator who makes something of no value. When we see the value of ourselves as His creation, we can rightfully honor and worship the Creator. This is the great reciprocal relationship of the Shulamite mentioned in chapter 1 of this book. She can love Him and others because she has received from Him something of great value to give.

**ACTIVATION:**

Beloved, who is He to you? Pour your heart out in loving adoration of your King and your friend. Think of His face, His arms, His heart, His legs, His feet. What characteristics of Jesus come to mind in each? Praise His beautiful nature that you have personally encountered, and this will be your own song to Him!

*"Where has your beloved gone, O most beautiful among women? Where has your beloved turned, that we may seek him with you?"*
*Song of Solomon 6:1*

The bride has just finished her own soliloquy on the beauty and majesty of the King, and the others around her are now convinced, through seeing into her heart, about His goodness.

They see the love and feel the conviction of the incorruptible love Paul speaks of in Ephesians 6:24. "Grace be with all who love our Lord Jesus Christ with a love incorruptible." He has satisfied her heart like no other, and others around her do not just hear her words but feel the depth of her sincere devotion. They long to know this kind of satisfaction in their own hearts.

As I was contemplating attending Bible college, I was pondering what I would study. Looking at the list of topics, my heart was drawn to evangelism. I watched a video of their trip the previous year to Mardi Gras where they traveled to share the hope of the gospel. Tears streamed down my face, and even though I could barely invite someone to church at this point in my life, I knew God was leading me here. On my first day of class, one of the women began to sob.

Several went to her side to console her and seek the Lord. This was not a worldly consolation to ease some kind of pain, but a spiritual comforting to seek the Lord about what He had put on her heart that caused the tears. I cried my own tears because I knew I had found where I belonged.

We began weekly outings into bustling downtown Dallas to share the gospel with the party-goers, wanderers, homeless, and others from many walks of life. My confidence began to increase as I experienced the exhilaration of overcoming the fear of sharing my faith. We approached people with love and genuine care, taking their prayer requests and offering our hand as we immediately petitioned Father God on their behalf. The lies I believed, including that people would not be receptive or that they would be offended, began to fall off, and I began to see their gratefulness for the hope shared. I later continued my evangelism journey with a nonprofit that equips local churches to go out beyond their building walls and share their faith with their community. I was now not only sharing hope with the destitute, but I was offering Jesus to people who were much more comfortable with their status in the world. I began to grow not only in my boldness through love, but I became more and more convinced of God's goodness toward me as the enemy's lies about my own value and purpose began to melt away. As I encountered Jesus at home, I could go out and tell others about the riches also available to them. This was a key part of my freedom. As I confessed Jesus with my mouth, I felt deeper and deeper levels of salvation.

*"If you confess with your mouth that Jesus is Lord and believe in your heart that God raised him from the dead, you will be saved" Romans 10:9.*

That word salvation is sozo (Strongs G4982), which is saved, delivered, protected, healed, and made whole. Jesus paid for me to experience all of this when He gave Himself on the cross, but my heart had to experience its reality to feel it and walk in greater faith. There is initial salvation, the free gift of Jesus, and there are deeper levels of salvation, also known as sanctification. These deeper levels have more to do with overcoming and victory in this life than they have to do with heaven and hell for eternity. Jesus's blood paid for us to experience realms of heaven now so that we can walk out our calling, plans, and purposes for Him in this life. As lies began falling off, I began to walk out freedom and joy like I never had experienced before.

**ACTIVATION:**

Beloved, who in your life needs hope? Start by asking them how you can pray for them, then pray with them. Feel the chains of silence fall off as you stand up for truth wherever you are. Don't beat yourself up if you cannot walk it out perfectly. Just keep walking...and sharing. He is with you always.

---

*"My beloved has gone down to his garden to the beds of spices, to graze in the gardens and to gather lilies. I am my beloved's and my beloved is mine; he grazes among the lilies."*
*Song of Solomon 6:2-3*

He never left, beloved. Sometimes, our hearts just need to be awakened to His presence. Worship has a way of aligning our hearts and minds with heaven; even though we are giving to Him, our hearts are also receiving the goodness of who He is. We do not need to remind a forgetful God or, worse, flatter a narcissistic God with pretty words. He is quite confident in who He is, but we benefit when we align our hearts with the truth of who He is. We as humans, who are constantly looking through our own self-centered viewpoint, often unconsciously assume

God is doing the same. He is not looking for us to build Him up; He is already Lord of all and can go no higher. There is no higher. However, He delights when His children speak truth so that they can enjoy the fullness within their own hearts of who He is.

When we use mechanical equipment the way it was intended, it works more efficiently. We are very similar in that when creation aligns with the Creator, our hearts begin to work properly. The way our hearts "work" dictates our steps, good or bad. We may worship Him, or we may sin.

Most define freedom as being able to make our own choices; this is a narrow view. With this definition, we can make many free-will choices that cause very grave consequences.

Those consequences, oftentimes, hinder life. God does not hinder life; God gives life abundantly (John 10:10). To help keep us from poor choices, God set two boundaries: to love God and love others *(Matthew 22:37-39)*. When we align ourselves with His law of love, we feel the freedom of righteousness and purity. When we align with Him, we have the freedom to choose what is right and life-giving.

Did you know that God is perfect and nothing can flaw Him? God is not even flawed by nearness to sin, but sin cannot stand next to our perfect Father. It melts like wax before Him. The craving of His heart is nearness to you. He craves, not just proximity to you, but internal communion with you. He has opened up the innermost Holy of Holy places to you through Jesus, and His desire is for you to allow Him into the very center of your heart as well. Beloved, you are His, and He is yours. He not only loves you, He likes you. Get comfortable with aligning your heart to this truth.

**ACTIVATION:**

Father, tell me what you like about me. Now listen…

---

*"You are beautiful as Tirzah, my love, lovely as Jerusalem, awesome as an army with banners. Turn away your eyes from me, for they overwhelm me." Song of Solomon 6:4-5*

Jesus wept over Jerusalem, the place of His Father's house. His heart was that every Jewish person would know Him and receive Him, for He knew the plan of redemption. He wept at the enemy's spiritual barricades around the city, which kept them from seeing the truth. He sees you like this beloved city. You are the place of His temple. "The hour is coming when neither on this mountain nor in Jerusalem will you worship the Father" *(John 4:21)*. You, beloved, are the temple worshiping in spirit and truth. When our adoring eyes meet His, He sees His desire manifested. Our gaze locks onto His, and the joy set before Him comes alive.

When the enemy steals our peace and our joy in knowing Him, He weeps. Consider His triumphal entry into Jerusalem *(Matthew 21)*. Our humble King rode upon a donkey and a colt, not the prestige of worldly kings' chariots. This is how He comes to our hearts. He is not forceful or arrogant, though some evangelists attempt this approach. He knows most of our hearts would recoil at force and arrogance. He comes gently, humbly, and only when invited.

*"Most of the crowd spread their cloaks on the road, and others cut branches from the trees and spread them on the road" Matthew 21:8.*

When we discover who He is, we lay down the welcome mats of our hearts to let Him in, and our eyes are opened to see our need for Him. *"Say to the daughter of Zion, 'Behold, your king is coming to you, humble, and mounted on a donkey, on a colt, the foal of a beast of burden" Matthew 21:5.*

Our King comes humbly for us, not afraid or ashamed of the enemy's work in our lives. *"For freedom Christ has set us free" Galatians 5:1.* He is the rescuer, beloved. He does not wait for you to clean up or get yourself out of the pit before He rescues you. The Rescuer comes into the deepest, darkest places to rescue His beloved. We don't clean up for Him; we need Him to get us cleaned up. I used to try to make myself worth loving. Now I know His love gives me my worth.

**ACTIVATION:**

Even at my weakest, my glance ravishes Him. He made it that way; He delights in you. Read those last two sentences again. Let that soak in.

---

*"Your teeth are like a flock of ewes that have come up from the washing; all of them bear twins; not one among them has lost its young. Your cheeks are like halves of a pomegranate behind your veil." Song of Solomon 6:6-7*

You may have noticed these lyrics the King sings over His bride repeat from chapter 4. Did you know the King never gets tired of repeating Himself? If you need to hear who you are in Him one more time or a million more times, He will tell you. The love chapter, 1 Corinthians 13, describes love. It describes our King because He is love. Jesus is patient and kind; He does not envy or boast; He is not arrogant or rude. He does not insist on His own way; He is not irritable or resentful; He does not rejoice at wrongdoing, but rejoices with the truth (1 Corinthians 13:4-6). He delights in truth and celebrates every time He tells us who we are. This is how I read the above verses: "Your smile is exhilarating to Me. The passion I feel when you look toward Me and feel satisfied in Me is indescribable." The Passion Translation® does an excellent job of dissecting these metaphors for modern readers so that we may receive these truths into our minds and hearts. I will not cover that here, but I encourage you to camp out next to that tent for a season; you will find riches there.

**ACTIVATION:**

Jesus, tell me again how You see me. What gold have You planted in me that you want to uncover? Let me have eyes to see, ears to hear, and a heart to receive.

---

*"My dove, my perfect one, is the only one, the only one of her mother, pure to her that bore her. The young women saw her and called her blessed; the queens and concubines also, and they praised her." Song of Solomon 6:9*

Mary, mother of Jesus, said, *"For behold, from now on all generations will call me blessed; for he who is mighty has done great things for me, and holy is his name" Luke 1:48-49.*

You are perfectly designed for the plans and purpose for which He created you. There is no one else like you, and if you do not carry His glory in the unique way in which He created you, no one else can. You are an expression of God's glorious nature that no one else can replicate. What has He created for you to birth in the earth? Even those next to earthly kings cannot match your royalty when you are walking out your God-given destiny. Even "queens and concubines", or fellow believers, will celebrate your journey. Because we are one body, we celebrate the body's success and champion our brothers and sisters.

As I began to grow in maturity in the Lord, I began to yearn to influence the world for His kingdom in bigger ways. As my confidence grew, the desires in my heart also grew to align with the coming journey. However, this growth was not without growing pains. At times, it was difficult to receive from female leadership, especially in my age group, because I longed to pour out what God had been working in me. In those moments, I would feel resentment and comparison. However, rather than yielding to these feelings, I cried out to Him to remove these feelings from me and to mold me, so that I could cheer on my sisters in Christ and receive from them. An important principle in the kingdom is that how we view others, we are likely to believe they view us the same way. At an even deeper level, we probably have the same feelings about ourselves burning undetected in our hearts. If I am not able to receive their message, when I have a message to share, I may subconsciously believe they cannot receive from me, hindering my own ministry.

The discipline of forgiveness works this way as well. When we cannot forgive, we often struggle with receiving forgiveness. When we cannot forgive, we have a core belief that certain faults or failures are beyond forgiveness, and we hinder ourselves from fully receiving forgiveness from the Father. Earlier in my journey, I began to have an urge to raise my hands in worship, which was not freely done at my church at that time. This seemed like an immovable block. In my quiet time, Jesus asked me to repent for knowingly or unknowingly judging anyone in their display of worship. Then, He asked me to forgive anyone who may have judged me in worship. This broke both sides of the block, and the next Sunday I raised my hands freely and with joy!

*"So also my heavenly Father will do to every one of you if you do not forgive your brother from your heart" Matthew 18:35.*

The word "do" (Strongs G4160) means to agree. When the wicked servant, who had been forgiven, showed what he believed about forgiveness, the Father agreed with him and put him in jail. That same word is in Matthew 7:12 and exemplifies this principle: *"So whatever you wish that others would do to you, do also to them."* This applies to our actions and our thoughts.

To free me of resentment and comparison, Jesus asked me to imagine putting the characters of one love story into a different love story. When I did, the story no longer worked because the personalities were different. It became a completely different story. We each have a love story with King Jesus and with our Father. We cannot insert ourselves into another's love story; if we do, it becomes a different story. He suggested to me that when the enemy comes with words of resentment or comparison, I should say, "Jesus, thank you for that person's love story with you. Thank you that they have a unique love story with you and so do I."

**ACTIVATION:**

Now it's your turn: Jesus, thank you for my unique love story with you. Forgive me for desiring another's story, and I forgive anyone who has not acknowledged my own story with You.

*"I went down to the nut orchard to look at the blossoms of the valley, to see whether the vines had budded, whether the pomegranates were in bloom. Before I was aware, my desire set me among the chariots of my kinsman, a prince."*
*Song of Solomon 6:11-12*

The Shulamite is beginning to believe that the King has been a faithful gardener in her heart. Rather than trying to earn His affection, she begins to walk out her faith with love and display the overflow of His heart within her. In Ephesians 2:8-9, Paul says that God's salvation is not a result of our works, but we are created to do good works prepared for us beforehand. This means that once we receive acceptance in Jesus, we can walk into the world, armed with His mercy and love, to do good works.

My quiet time, reading the Bible, and speaking to Jesus, was inconsistent until the morning I decided to replace watching the morning news with reading the scripture. This time became a priority for me, but I didn't shame myself for missing it. I began to journal about my reading and then gradually added more time as my hunger increased. I began to have more unusual encounters with Him. For example, at times, I felt those warm chills down my back.

Another time, I smelled a mysterious scent like strawberry air freshener, which was not obnoxious but quite enticing. The scent left quickly, but I still remember it today. I couldn't account for it in any of my surroundings as there were no candles, air fresheners, or anything that would emit fragrance.

These mornings with the King were like getting to know a best friend. As my inner-healing journey began, I incorporated these experiences into my quiet time. Many of my healing encounters with Jesus happened in my quiet time, just as they did in sessions with a minister. These encounters were like visiting the garden of my heart and grazing among the fruit planted by the King. As I showed up morning after morning, my intimacy with Him increased. I sought Him more throughout the day and also in the evening. My other daily routines began to fall into place, and no time was lost. Many previous activities no longer seemed important; the necessary tasks became a joy. I used to feel annoyed at small things, such as filling the coffee maker with water, which seemed to take forever and created a dripping mess on the counter. I used to clench and grind my teeth at night so much that the dentist suggested a mouth guard to keep my teeth from continuing to wear down. I used to bite my nails. I used to take medication because I suffered from depression. I used to control everyone around me so that my life would "go well." Day by day, the Lord gently healed me, pulling it away layer by layer.

Several years ago, I was sick on the couch with the flu for two weeks. I spent my time praying, reading the Bible and devotionals, watching Bible movies, and praying. In prayer, I cried out to God to change my husband so we could have a good marriage. I had prayed this many times, but, this time, I heard so clearly, "Why are you asking me to change him when I'm trying to change you?" At that moment, a gentle conviction fell over me, and my heart posture changed. I still prayed for my marriage, but I allowed myself to become more malleable to the Lord's molding. While trying to feed my ravenous soul, I looked up and found my Prince. He wants the hearts of our family and friends, but, beloved, He wants all of yours as well. My eyes turned from winning the approval of my husband to gazing upon the One who could fulfill me.

**ACTIVATION:**

Jesus, forgive me when my eyes look to others. I love them better when I love You first. Holy Spirit, show me how to love You well, and fill me to overflowing.

*"Return, return, O Shulammite, return, return, that we may look upon you. [He:] Why should you look upon the Shulammite, as upon a dance before two armies?" Song of Solomon 6:13*

As we see other Shulamites in the kingdom, we glean from their love stories with Jesus. They tell us what He looks like to them and to the depths that they have searched Him; but, the King desires your eyes upon Him. When Jacob sees the angels of God in Genesis 32:2, he names the land Mahanaim, which means two armies or two camps. The king is telling us that we must not exalt, or look upon, the experience of others above our own revelation with the Lord. We must not rely solely on sermons and religious books outside of God's word to feed us. These are great for guidance but a poor substitute for real spiritual food from the Lord.

I received a prescription for real spiritual food in my first freedom session with my mentor at the time. I was at an evangelism event where I had an experience that was outside my spiritual understanding. While I attended Bible college, I was not prepared for a physical attack by the enemy. So, when I felt the enemy physically upon me, I did what I knew to do: I went into the worship service, dropped to my knees, and lifted my hands in praise. I cried out for God to take it. I commanded it to go. Nothing worked. I knew I could not go a minute more with this torment.

As my mentor sat quietly reading his Bible, I approached him apologetically. When he led me to a cafe table in the lobby, I began to cry and shake. In response, he found another female to join our session in a private room. As I began to explain my plight, I let out a cough. He looked at me and asked if something was trying to come out or if I had a cough. "I don't have a cough," I answered. After several violent coughing bouts and numerous demons leaving, I felt the weightiness of peace so heavily that I ended up laid out on the floor. As I lay there, he prophesied over me the Song of Solomon and suggested I read it in The Passion Translation® some inconceivable number of times. I had recently found this book in a local thrift store, so Jesus had already provided the means. I prayed, all the way home, that the feeling of that glory would not leave, and it didn't. That night, I laid down to sleep in the greatest peace I had known in my life.

**ACTIVATION:**

Jesus, lead me out of the box of my comfort for my freedom and for Your glory. I want to experience more of you. Get anything out of the way that keeps me from a deeper journey with You. Reveal plots of the enemy that hinder me so I can experience the fullness of Your peace.

*"How beautiful are your feet in sandals, O noble daughter! Your rounded thighs are like jewels, the work of a master hand. Your navel is a rounded bowl that never lacks mixed wine. Your belly is a heap of wheat, encircled with lilies." Song of Solomon 7:1-2*

The Shulamite is learning she is a noble daughter!

Verse 7 is full of metaphors that describe her heavenly identity. Her spiritual belly is full of provision *(Song of Sol. 7:2)*; she is a mother in the faith and able to feed those new in the faith. She looks intently at her King with an unwavering face (Song of Sol. 7:4); she is not swayed by other doctrines or persecution, and her eyes see healing where others just see hurt. She is crowned as a queen in royalty in the kingdom of heaven *(Song of Sol. 7:5)*; earthly kings are in troughs or ditches compared to the heavenly status of Jesus's beloveds. Her heart is like the clusters of a palm tree *(Song of Sol. 7:7)*, with coconut meat and milk to nurture others.

We may smile at the silliness of the metaphors, but discipleship is a real need in the kingdom. We need people to tell us who we are according to God so we can live from this heavenly identity. I was not raised in church. When I was in middle school, a local Baptist church began picking my sister and me up by bus to attend Sunday School. After a few months, I was intrigued by the leader's call for us to accept Jesus, so I raised my hand. I ended up in another room across the hall with a young lady sharing Jesus's offer of sacrifice for me. I liked the idea of His offering, and I said my prayer. My excitement dwindled quickly, though, because the bus stopped picking us up for reasons unknown, and no one taught me what to do with my newfound faith. Without discipleship, I put it on a shelf and went about life. I went on to make many poor choices before reconfirming my faith as an adult.

For years, I shared my testimony with others that I was saved at age 30. However, one day during a worship service, the Lord reminded me of that day at the Baptist church. As I remembered, he asked, "Do you think I would just turn my back on an offering of your heart?

Do you think I crossed my arms and said, 'That's not good enough?'" As tears streamed down my face, I realized I had been His for so much longer. I encountered the goodness of His mercy, His grace, and His humility. *"Truly, I say to you, today you will be with me in paradise" Luke 23:43*. What did the thief say to get such esteem? *"Jesus, remember me" Luke 23:42.*

He didn't have theology, obedience, or water baptism. His heart called upon the Lord that day, and Jesus met him with mercy and love. He received a 13-year-old me when I had no idea of what I was giving but a simple, heartfelt yes to His offer. It was as if I said, "Remember me," and He said, "I thought you'd never ask."

**ACTIVATION:**

When did you tell Jesus, "Remember me"? Reminisce with Him, and ask Him what He thinks about it. I feel Him smiling already.

*"I am my beloved's, and his desire is for me."*
*Song of Solomon 7:10*

The simplicity of this verse makes it one of my favorites. Notice the Shulamite is confessing her conviction of His love and desire for her. He has reminded her who she is, and she is coming into agreement with Him. This is the revelation of John. Have you ever thought it presumptuous that he would call himself the one whom Jesus loved *John 13:23*)?

I do not think He was boasting; I think he caught a revelation of Jesus's perfect love. He came into agreement with Jesus's extraordinary love for him. He was the one who laid his head upon the Son of God's chest *(John 13:23)*, and the one who stayed at the cross *(John 19:26)*. Beloved, I stress again that when we agree with the beauty that Jesus sees in us, our hearts and minds see the beauty of who He is as well. When you know you're loved, you will give your life for that love. Jesus said, "Greater love has no one than this, that someone lay down his life for his friends" (John 15:13). Martyrdom is not for duty or merit, but for love. The Psalmist implores, *"Keep me as the apple of your eye; hide me in the shadow of your wings" (Psalm 17:8)*. Jesus knew He was the apple of His Father's eye. Because of this perfect unity, He was able to carry out all that the Father laid before Him for His glory and out of love for us.

Jesus paid the price for us to come boldly to the Father, and He delights in us. Because of this, we have access to the Father. I have had numerous visions in the throne room of God. These were simple visions that happened when I allowed Jesus to speak to me by showing me visions of the Father's throne. Many times the throne room had details He placed there just for me. When He had been speaking to me about sapphires in the Bible, I saw the whole throne room blue, including the elders! I love the ocean, so for a long time, I saw an ocean rolling up into the sea of glass before Him.

One time, I saw myself as a little girl playing with blocks on the steps before Him. When I asked Him about this, He told me that my things were kept there because it was my home, too. I cried tears of joy at such welcoming acceptance by the One who is above all. Give Jesus any lies about the Father that might hinder you from seeing Him, and ask Jesus to take you to see His Father. He paid for that, beloved. The Father sent His Son because He desired communion with you.

**ACTIVATION:**

Jesus, are there any lies I'm believing about the Father that would hinder me from seeing Him clearly? I give that lie to you. Will you take me to see your Father?

---

*"Beside our doors are all choice fruits, new as well as old, which I have laid up for you, O my beloved." Song of Solomon 7:13*

I have never had much success with growing fruits and vegetables in my yard, but I have had the pleasure of enjoying the abundance from a friend or neighbor. Imagine that you had grown an abundance of produce and placed it at your door for your neighbors to swap freely.

Do you allow Jesus to use your abundance freely? There is new fruit, beloved, but there is also older fruit, which is revelation from my painful past. I have shared some of my older abundance here, and I am not ashamed. Jesus has gone to every painful memory I can possibly remember and taken out every wound, lie, and sting until any traumatic memory is dead in my heart. Now that the enemy cannot use it to hurt me, my story is a testimony of Jesus's mercy, kindness, and grace.

When I took an evangelism class at the Bible college, the teacher challenged us with an assignment to write a three-minute testimony that described where we had been and how we met Jesus. I knew I had made some choices in my life that had opened the door to the enemy and were critical to seeing the grace of Jesus in my life. The problem was that I had not told anyone about these past choices. As far as I was concerned, these were bottled-up secrets that I believed could stay secret. However, with this assignment, I knew it was time to let it all out.

The enemy loves for us to hide and keep secrets, but, when all is brought to the light, the enemy no longer has control. This simple act of confession to others brought amazing freedom to my heart. Personal sins can be simply confessed to God and forgiven; but, we should not hesitate to share about the forgiveness and grace we have received if Jesus is opening a door for us to help someone else in need of our story. In fact, we know we have received healing in an area when we can have a thankful heart for what was once a hurtful memory. This does not mean we are glad it happened, but we are grateful for God's healing and delight in Him allowing our story to help others. This is a sign that a thankful heart has been cultivated within us. This older fruit not only benefits others but benefits us as well.

"We are more than conquerors through Him who loved us" *(Romans 8:37)*. As conquerors, we win the battle. As more than conquerors, we take what the enemy meant for evil, and allow God to use it for our good and the good of others. I caution you not to blame God for the evil of the world. We have a real enemy that has made a career of wreaking havoc in the lives of God's children. I believe most of God's discipline is simply His redirection because the enemy is so quick to make us pay for our mistakes. I have seen Him turn evil for the benefit of His children time and time again.

**ACTIVATION:**

Jesus, I give you every dark memory and invite your goodness into it. I open those places to You that I have not wanted anyone to see.

*Oh that you were like a brother to me who nursed at my mother's breasts! If I found you outside, I would kiss you, and none would despise me...His left hand is under my head, and his right hand embraces me! I adjure you, O daughters of Jerusalem, that you not stir up or awaken love until it pleases." Song of Solomon 8:1, 3-4*

Have you ever met someone who started strong in their faith, but who also experienced a bit of backlash and then quickly retreated back, almost to the place they were before they ever met Jesus? I once met a store clerk who said he had followed Jesus and began immediately going out to share his faith, wearing Jesus t-shirts every day; but, he didn't like the persecution he experienced, so he threw away the t-shirts and his faith. Oh, I desire that everyone saw following Jesus as a glorious life calling and could kiss Him in front of the world! I believe Jesus is still embracing that man who has decided Jesus is not worth the cost.

When I first recommitted my life to Jesus, I was so excited about the joy I felt in my heart. At a family gathering, I began to share my experience with a family member, and I was immediately barraged with hurtful words that I was judging and pushy. My heart felt crushed.

All of the love, joy, and excitement that I wanted to share with this person quickly fizzled in that moment. I didn't share my faith again for quite some time. In fact, as I mentioned, I was hesitant to even invite someone to church. But Jesus kept His loving arms around me, drawing me closer to His side, as I continued to pursue Him. Through the years, I have experienced other persecution from family and friends, even pastors and church members. Some of it was overt, and some of it simply felt like I was being "too much." I acknowledge some of it could have been the enemy's lies filtering into my thoughts, but the awkwardness, avoidance, resentment, and making fun of me were very real at times. Nonetheless, I knew what Jesus had done in my heart, and I could no longer deny His truth and my inner freedom. The more I sat with Him and drew closer to Him, the closer He drew to me until compassion arose within me for those without hunger. I became more and more unapologetic, but I stayed tethered to Jesus in love as well.

I am not advocating that new followers not engage in great feats of obedience for the kingdom, but, when you do, remain steadfast. Do not expect even your own family to understand. "For from now on in one house there will be five divided, three against two and two against three" (Luke 12:52). I held back my pursuit of Jesus for a season in an attempt to please my family. I had one eye on Jesus and one eye on everyone else; I was blocking my own freedom. We do not have to display an intentional boldness to cause such division; the pursuit of His truth even in gentleness and care may be divisive. Jesus is the fountain that allows us to love and care for others without expectation. My love awakened as I discovered His character and who He truly is. Once we know this, the affection we carry for Him cannot help but pour out on all who are around us.

**ACTIVATION:**

Jesus, thank you for being patient with me as I grow in knowing you more. Show me the places where I have my eyes on the world and people around me and not on You. I give you permission to hold my face toward Yours. I want to view others through the lens of your love and freedom.

*"Who is that coming up from the wilderness, leaning on her beloved? Under the apple tree I awakened you. There your mother was in labor with you; there she who bore you was in labor with you." Song of Solomon 8:5*

I would like to emphasize "leaning on her beloved," not "coming from the wilderness." Life will bring you wilderness after wilderness, and some seasons will be easier than others; but, there are some who never seem to see the ease because they constantly focus on the difficult.

Did you know that God blesses you in different ways? He may give or He may take away to guide us. If we are aware and ask Him, He will reveal the blessing He is trying to give us instead. I wasn't thrilled with my new job at a retail store when my heart's desire was to minister. Honestly, I never pictured myself as a 40-something store clerk. I see now that that was quite pompous of me. That job was a blessing. Not only did I obtain enough job history to purchase a new vehicle, but God began bringing people from my past, some friends and others from hurtful church experiences, into the store. God was gracious in the order He brought them into the store. By the time I saw people who hurt me from the church, Jesus had cultivated a thankful heart within me for my job; and I was able to serve with a smile and without a pang of bitterness or embarrassment. I felt free. Freedom was God's blessing, and I could have missed it had I continued resenting the job. When the job felt like a wilderness, I clung to my Beloved. I still have wildernesses going on in life, but now I forget about them much of the time.

There are deep pains that happen in life, but that is why leaning on the Beloved must be the emphasis. The Old Testament introduces us to Job, a man that is probably most known for his suffering. Although Job had his faults of blaming God and focusing on his own good deeds to save himself from the pain *(Job 27:6)*, he kept returning to the acknowledgment of God being the answer *(Job 19:25-27)*. He ultimately sought a relationship with God (Job 42:4), knowing every answer he needed would be found in the One who was before time and always will be.

He clung, at times with a twisted grip, to his Beloved, and he received his desire. God spoke with him. He had the One who is awe and wonder before his eyes, and only then was Job speechless. When he can speak again, Job is able to acknowledge that God has given him the relationship he longed for; *"Hear, and I will speak; I will question you, and you make it known to me" (Job 42:4)*. He can have the conversation with the Father that he earlier raged about not having.

*"I had heard of you by the hearing of the ear, but now my eye sees you" Job 42:5.*

Only then does Job even realize the endearment "Beloved." Job repents for having any other vision about his God, letting go of other notions of who He is. The wilderness is not a place of ease in life; it is a place of peace in relationship with Jesus. It is not a place of ignoring problems by saying, "It's fine. Everything's fine." It's more than fine; it's thriving because of the life within you that doesn't dull from circumstances. It is allowing Him to acknowledge you, laying your life story before Him (as hurtful as it may be), and receiving His grace that changes you forever *(see Luke 8:43-48*).

Remember tasting His goodness in Song of Solomon 2:3? Your Beloved is the apple tree in the fruitless forest of the world. You delighted in His shadow. Now in verse 8:5, He says this is where you were awakened. This is where you came alive! You were created for this life with Him, trampling scorpions and crushing the heads of snakes *(Luke 10:19)*. The enemy may meet you in the wilderness. He met Jesus in the wilderness as well *(Matthew 4:1-11, Mark 1:12-13, Luke 4:1-13)*. But we have Him as our blessed hope! I see a vision of Jesus swinging out of the trees from a vine like Tarzan, and Jane, the bride, is clinging to Him. May it be for us as well, beloved; never let go!

**ACTIVATION:**

Where is the hurt and frustration in your life right now? Jesus, I give it to you. If the touch of Your garment heals, how much more if I abide in Your presence! What is the blessing You want me to see in my circumstances?

---

*"Set me as a seal upon your heart, as a seal upon your arm, for love is strong as death, jealousy is fierce as the grave. Its flashes are flashes of fire, the very flame of the Lord."*
*Song of Solomon 8:6*

Seals were often made with a piece of wax being stamped with a signet (ring or necklace) to make a unique image representing its owner. Like in the book of Esther, we usually think of kings making decrees and then sealing them with their signet ring, deeming them irreversible. Judah, one of the sons of Jacob and one of the tribes of Israel, was not a king, but he had a signet as a necklace. This could have been used to enter into agreements and mark his belongings.

Let's explore Judah's signet. In Genesis 38, Judah promised his widowed daughter-in-law Tamar that he would provide his young son for her when the son is of age, as was the Jewish tradition. Later, when she sees that the son is of age, she takes off her widow clothing and puts on "a veil, wrapping herself up" (Genesis 38:14). Judah, however, does not approach her as his daughter-in-law but as a prostitute. He doesn't recognize her; her hopes are dashed. Instead of confronting Judah, Tamar plays the harlot. Judah offers to send payment later, and she requests collateral: his staff, bracelet (or cord), and signet. These three items were unique in identifying Judah among his people. When Judah's friends show up with the payment, she vanishes and reemerges in his hometown. Rumors reach Judah that she is "pregnant by immorality" *(Genesis 38:24*). He calls for her to be burned, but she presents his personal belongings before them and incriminates Judah as well. He humbles himself, saying;

*"She is more righteous than I, since I did not give her to my son Shelah" Genesis 38:26.*

Fast forward, beloved, to John 8. The scribes and Pharisees bring an adulterous woman before Jesus, recommending she be stoned for her sin. Can you see Judah and his friends bringing Tamar before Jesus? Scripture then tells us Jesus wrote something in the dirt *(John 8:6)*. He then tells whoever has never sinned to throw the first stone, and He writes something else in the dirt. After that, the older ones left first followed by the younger ones.

I visited those stories to bring you here. Jesus said, "Woman, where are they? Has no one condemned you?" *(John 8:10)* It was as if Jesus held the staff, cords, and signet of every scribe and Pharisee who brought the accused woman forth. When confronted, they did not respond with Judah's humility, even though they had the opportunity. As Judah withheld his son from Tamar, these scribes and Pharisees withheld the truth of the scriptures from their people.

Standing in front of Jesus, they withheld the truth He came to provide in the form of eternal life and freedom. They left with their sin still intact because their eyes were on her sin and trying to hide their own. Her sin was forgiven because she was confronted, and her eyes were on Jesus.

Today, Jesus holds the signet of our identity. He knows who we were created to be and our purpose. When we stop hiding our own faults and lay them at His feet, we allow His stamp upon our hearts, much like Judah's hung around his neck close to his heart.

Jesus places the ring of bridal promise on our finger and calls us sons and daughters. Like the prodigal son, He meets us on the road and sees our surrendered hearts *(Luke 15:11-32)*. The Father waits on the porch of heaven for you, beloved! As soon as your heart begins to awaken in repentance of living in lesser places, His heart feels the spark of awakening, and He takes off down the road to meet you. How precious you are to Him, beloved. He trusts you with not only His authority to represent His kingdom on earth, but He expects that you'll stamp His insignia on His belongings, which is all of creation, fulfilling our role as ministers of reconciliation.

*"All this is from God, who through Christ, reconciled us to himself and gave us the ministry of reconciliation" 2 Corinthians 5:18.*

If death and the grave are sure to our mortal bodies on this earth, how much more sure is His love and desire for our whole heart? If the enemy's work is inevitable in this life, take heart, beloved, because your Rescuer has overcome the world to blaze a trail for you! "Whoever receives his testimony sets his seal to this, that God is true" *(John 3:33).* The Passion Translation® states John 3:33 this way: *"Yet those who embrace his message know in their hearts that it's the truth."* When you settle in your heart the truth of the Beloved, you are sealed as His very own and sent out in the world as His representative—His brother, His sister, His bride!

**ACTIVATION:**

Jesus, I hand you all shame and condemnation today. You know everything about me, and that frees me. I receive Your full forgiveness so I am released to fully represent you. I receive Your full forgiveness so that there is nothing hindering the fullness of relationship with You.

*"Many waters cannot quench love, neither can floods drown it. If a man offered for love all the wealth of his house, he would be utterly despised." Song of Solomon 8:7*

If love is the flame of the Lord *(Song of Sol. 8:6)*, there is nothing that can put it out. Jesus was and is a master at fanning the flame in our hearts. We read about His encounters with various people in scripture that ignited the fire of their hearts, and He seemed to respond to each differently. To the rich young ruler, He advised him to sell everything and follow Him *(Matthew 19:16-22, Mark 10:17-27, Luke 18:1823)*. In this encounter, when the ruler uses the word "good," Jesus immediately redirects him to the Father. When he asks, "What must I do?" the ruler reveals his belief that he himself must accomplish it. Jesus responds by offering up a few of the commandments to which the ruler quickly responds that he has kept them since he was a boy.

I believe he was having this exchange with Jesus because he knew something was missing. He was accomplished, but his pages of accomplishments could never buy what is given for free. Mark's account says, *"And Jesus, looking at him, loved him" (Mark 10:21)*. The same verse in the King James version says, *"Jesus beholding him loved him."* It was as if they were having a casual conversation that suddenly became serious, and Jesus peered into his eyes with love so he could receive the freedom of life that was right before his eyes. Jesus responds, *"You lack one thing: go, sell all that you have and give to the poor, and you will have treasure in heaven; and come, follow me"* Mark 10:2.

Are we as believers called to give up all our possessions to be perfect in our own strength? No, beloved, only communion with the King can do that for us. Jesus might have said, "If you want your heart satisfied or if you want life and life abundant then go and sell all you have and follow me." Jesus didn't have his eye on the young man's possessions; Jesus had his eye on his heart. The young man was looking at his accomplishments, and one of them was his great wealth. One of the commandments Jesus didn't mention in their previous exchange is having no idols in our hearts before God. This is not a narcissistic demand from a wrathful god, but this is a loving boundary from a good Father who knows our hearts and how we were created. He knows that when He is on the throne of our hearts, all other priorities will fall into place. It's not that things will be less important; it means they will not grip our hearts and bind us to their success or failure in an unhealthy way. The enemy loves for us to get value from things other than Jesus because when those things are removed or fail, we feel broken. When our value is received only from Jesus, we will love our family better, we will be more trustworthy with friends, and we will be more productive at work. His hand of grace will be on everything we do in partnership with Him.

A couple of years ago, my son and I heard from the Lord that we would be moving to a new state. We both received confirmation after confirmation, so we packed up everything but the necessities in our house. We were waiting on God to open the door with a home and a job, or a clear directional word for the next step. As we got further in this process, reality set in.

I had two younger daughters still living at home and they both said that they would choose to stay with their dad rather than move with us. I was crushed. I didn't know what I had expected, really, but I had hoped their dad would move as well. In the subsequent tug of war in my soul and after much crying out to God, I conceded that I would go if that's what He had for me. When I made this decision, it felt like a rope that had been pulling me suddenly snapped. I realized my children, all of them, had been idols in my heart, keeping me from putting Jesus first. In my heart, I wanted love and acceptance from my children more than Jesus. Beloved, no one consciously believes this in their mind. It was buried deep in my heart where only Jesus could see, and He wanted all of me. "The heart is deceitful above all things, and desperately sick; who can understand it? 'I the LORD search the heart and test the mind" *(Jeremiah 17:9-10)*. I never moved to a new state. I have put that word on a shelf and believe God may still have a plan for it. I don't have all the answers, but I know He does. I'm grateful for the way my heart grew closer to Him in that season. Now, I have a more healthy attachment to my children the way God intended.

I cannot tell you if the young man actually needed to sell all his belongings. I believe if he had, he would have reached the remedy for his lack. He would have had to reach for the Provider of all things and cultivate a relationship of trust with Him. God does not call every believer to live a life of poverty to prove his or her spirituality, but He may call us to give up something that is sitting on His throne in our hearts. Song of Solomon 8:7 says that if he offered all he had for love, he'd be despised. Love is what he needed.

**ACTIVATION:**

Jesus, I give you permission to uncover any idols I have in my heart above You. I cannot fix the priorities in my heart, but You can. I declare Your Lordship over my heart, and I ask You to lead me through the processes to follow you completely.

*"We have a little sister, and she has no breasts. What shall we do for our sister on the day when she is spoken for? If she is a wall, we will build on her a battlement of silver, but if she is a door, we will enclose her with the boards of cedar."*
*Song of Solomon 8:8-9*

Throughout the Song of Solomon, the Shulamite had "others" following her journey, perhaps a circle of friends, who were watching this love affair unfold. They wanted to rejoice with her, watch her, and question her about her Beloved. Yet, He was always her Beloved. As we walk out our maturing in Jesus, others will be watching, intentionally or not. They will see the tough moments in the valleys and the moments of rejoicing on the mountains. We start the trek with Jesus, imagining the beautiful story He will write with us. It is a beautiful story, but it may have twists and turns of rejection, persecution, and misunderstanding that we were not expecting. If you live a bold life for Jesus, those times will surely come. As the onlookers choose their own journey with the King, we may feel tempted to protect others from such a bumpy ride. Discipling others is a healthy kingdom activity. We want to humbly share the revelation we have acquired at His feet so that our ceiling is the floor for others for the glory of the Father. Parents, especially, want to shield their children from the woes of life. However, what if the bumpy ride of the tough seasons is what drives them to His arms, making His love and comfort more real than anything they can physically see? The Shulamite seems to quell their fears by saying,

*"I was in his eyes as one who finds peace"—Song of Solomon 8:10.*

Beloved, do you have friends or family who have not yet decided to allow the King into their hearts or who have not fully surrendered to His goodness and lordship? In His graciousness, Jesus has provided me with what I like to call "visions of promise." These are visions of others that the Lord has given me. In one vision, I see a young lady dancing in a bridal gown with Jesus. They are in a ballroom and dancing together like a newlywed couple's first dance. My heart swells with joy when I see the smile on her face and her eyes mesmerized by His. In another vision, I see a child nestled on the lap of Jesus, with her head on his chest.

They are sitting on a large rock, and His arms hold her close. In yet another one, I see a young woman beautifully dressed in a white draping gown with a gold sash. Her hair is swept up, and her entire body glistens with gold dust. Her arms are stretched outward, and she gazes up into the heavens. I also have had one of a young man who is in a carpenter shop with Jesus. As Jesus crafts His woodwork, the young man peers intently. At times, the young man is doing the work, and Jesus is guiding him.

When situations seem hopeless, I can visit those visions. Through them, the Lord reminds me that His plans are good, and He has not forgotten His promises. Even the good father in the parable of the prodigal son allowed his son to explore the empty passions of the world, before he welcomed him home. The road may look bumpy now, but His hand of love follows them and throws out seeds to mark a path that will eventually lead them right to His heart. Don't despise the journey for yourself or for others. As I said before, aren't we thankful Jesus doesn't mind being the God of last resort? Many of us only reached for Him after we ran our inheritance dry and ended up yearning for spiritual food at the pig farm of the world.

**ACTIVATION:**

Jesus, I lay those who are dear to me before You. Use the love I pour out to them to reveal Yourself to them and guide them in the way that will bring them into Your arms. Jesus, may I have a vision of promise to hold in my heart to remind me of Your goodness for them?

*Solomon had a vineyard at Baal-hamon; he let out the vineyard to keepers; each one was to bring for its fruit a thousand pieces of silver. My vineyard, my very own, is before me; you, O Solomon, may have the thousand, and the keepers of the fruit two hundred." Song of Solomon 8:11-12*

Jesus has a vineyard in each of our hearts, and as more enter the kingdom, a symphony of tribes, tongues, and nations come together for His praise. Beloved, He has torn the veil so that you can enter His holiest of holy places. You never have to fear, and you, beautiful child, can run right in with your muddy feet, poor choices, and questions and doubts. Jesus is the God who washes feet, cleanses hearts, and quietens souls. He is asking you to come. And when you see the ever-flowing goodness from this majestic and holy God, may your knees buckle, your face plant to the floor, and your arms stretch out in surrender before His righteous throne. He welcomes you, and the closer you get to Him, the more awe and wonder will fill you until you are unconscious of other lovers.

Earlier in my inner-healing journey, God allowed me to encounter Him in such a way that words will never fully convey it. I can only describe what God showed me that day, and I hope in my vulnerability, you are blessed. Like Paul described a man in 2 Corinthians 12:2, whether I was in or out of the body, I do not know. I am not sure if I was on earth or in heaven. My physical body sat on my couch during my morning quiet time with Jesus, but the visions were so intense I was oblivious to the natural and earthly time. Eight different scenes took me from shy uncertainty to elated bridal confidence with the Father. I understand that the Song of Solomon seems to present Jesus as the Beloved Bridegroom, as do other places in scripture, but in these encounters, I envisioned the Father.

Though the Trinity is one God, they are three distinct entities to me, and each represents a unique facet of God Himself. These are tender experiences that I realize many might not share, but I believe God has given me the grace to share these so that others may experience Him deeply in a unique way. I will not share every precious detail or every scene here, but I will give you a taste of the experience with five scenes.

My first encounter was in a medieval-looking castle. The walls looked like they were made of cinder blocks, and there were knights in armor next to the doors. The Father and I sat at opposite ends of a very long dining table. In these visions, I could not see His face, and I could barely see a trace of skin on His hands. I believe with Jesus's Spirit in us, we can see God, including His face, and any way He wants to present Himself to us because we are made righteous under the New Covenant.

However, I did not see His face this time. I looked shyly His way, and He, boldly yet gently, insisted I sit closer. With Him on the end and me at the corner by His side, we were served dinner. I was in such awe of His presence that I could not eat! After He ate, I hoped it would not end, so I asked what would be next. "Dessert," He had replied with a smile. I was still unable to eat, so He playfully dabbed some of the dessert on my nose. Joy. Even now, I cannot write these words without experiencing the emotion all over again with tears in my eyes.

The scene then changed. We walked out to a sea of people that reminded me of a display of the royal family in England. He encouraged me to greet as many people as I could by hugging them, shaking their hands, smiling, and encouraging them. He was doing the same. His eyes kept meeting mine as He must have known my need for encouragement. His face beamed with delight.

Next, we sat atop a Ferris wheel. The cars were candy apple red with gold lettering. He sat on my left. I gazed out at a sky that was so bright with clouds and light. As I looked out, His eyes were on me. Then I looked at Him and back out upon His kingdom. Tears filled my eyes as I soaked in His delight at me enjoying His creation. He made me feel as though all of it was made for me. Biblically I know that everything was made through and for Jesus *(Colossians 1:16)*, but isn't that like our generous God, to make us know we are the apple of His eye?

Back at the castle, we stood face to face before a large roaring fireplace. My humble King bent on one knee and opened a small red velvet ring box. Inside was a ring with a large red heart that was cut like a gem. At that moment, I knew supernaturally that I had all three of the Trinity there. The Father was on His knee, the red heart represented Jesus, and the roaring fire was the Holy Spirit. Humbled by such intimate majesty, I am not sure how I did not melt into a puddle before Him. I graciously took the ring, barely able to see it through my tears, and pulled it toward me where it sunk into my chest.

Next, we were standing hand in hand looking at a perfectly green hill crowned with a white stone building with dark wood trim. I wore a white flowing dress. We walked the short path to the entrance where pews lined both sides and the path continued in the middle. In awe, I realized I was a bride! People sat at every pew, and they stood as we entered. Their faces beamed as if they knew the joy of the moment for themselves. I remember wondering who could marry me to God? As soon as the curiosity came, I saw Jesus at the end of the path! All of us held hands, but I could not stand in the awe anymore. I dropped to my knees with my face drenched in thankful tears. Jesus and the Father knelt with me, and the tears came even more furiously than before. A bubble glistened around us—the Holy Spirit—and I never felt unity and love more overwhelmingly in my life. Afterward, He told me He would spend eternity courting me and winning my love.

A God who gave all and paid for all will never stop showing us how much He loves us—ever. Beloved, if He leaves the 99 to pursue the one (Matthew 18:12), may we never, for all of eternity, stop being "the one." May we never tire of His pursuit of our hearts, and may we always yield to this worthy King what is rightfully His.

**ACTIVATION:**

Beloved, ask the King where He would like to meet you. When you begin to see a scene in your mind, look for Him there, be with Him there. Or, start with a scene described above. Envision it, and invite Him into it. Let your heart fully embrace His presence and His love for you. Don't rush this moment with the King of Kings.

*"[He:] O you who dwell in the gardens, with companions listening for your voice; let me hear it.*
*[She:] Make haste my beloved, and be like a gazelle or a young stag on the mountains of spices." Song of Solomon 8:13-14*

Oh, I remember the journey of the Shulamite adoring her King in chapter 2. Now, another maiden has joined her hungry heart to His and invited Jesus over the mountains of protection in her heart to experience a freedom that she's never yet known. Let Him hear your voice, beloved!

**ACTIVATION:**

Jesus, I don't want to miss any gift You have for me on the table in my life. I want every part of my heart to be fully yours, and I give You permission to lead me on this Shulamite journey that will continue forever.

## Holy Echo

*Your songs of love*
*Drip into my heart*
*Until every part*
*Of You fills me,*
*And I receive*
*My identity*
*As the one You desire.*

*Your delight*
*Convinces my soul*
*Of what I've been told.*
*The sword of Ancient Text*
*Reaches the point of intersect.*
*God plus man perfect.*
*I am the one You desire.*

*Your sacred serenade*
*Woos my heart to agree*
*That I can run free,*
*Living out Your prophecy.*
*You're the Creator of eternity*
*Singing as You knitted me.*
*I was always Your desire.*

*The King's melody*
*Tends my garden with love,*
*Multiplying fruit from above.*
*I call to the High Priest*
*To come in and feast*
*In His temple that is me.*
*I revel in being His desire.*

*I must sing my song*
*To a Perfect Prince*
*Who first gave me His kiss.*
*The veil of His temple was torn*
*To clean away scorn.*
*I am His sheep newly shorn.*
*I sing to Him, My Desire.*

*Our song carries out*
*On display to the brides.*
*Love rolls in as tides,*
*The Holy of Holies in my soul*
*A constant washing bowl*
*Where the enemy's lost his toll.*
*Others come to feel His desire.*

*Our affections poured out,*
*A ballad He sings;*
*My praises I bring.*
*A holy echo goes forth,*
*A destiny in birth*
*To love Him first.*
*He is my desire.*

## Author Bio

Rhonda Michelle Smith is a Christian author, speaker, and host of the Pierced by Love Podcast. She helps people discover deeper intimacy with God through embracing their God-given identity. As founder of the nonprofit Pierced by Love, she's passionate about guiding others into transformative friendship with Jesus.

Through her own journey of healing from childhood sexual abuse, deep rejection, and the aftermath of trauma, Rhonda found freedom in Christ's love. Now she empowers others to experience that same breakthrough and live with purpose.

Rhonda's mission is simple: help everyone discover how deeply God loves them and how clearly His voice speaks into their daily lives.

You can purchase more books at PiercedByLove.com on our resources page or on Amazon.com.

For more information on Rhonda's ministry business, Pierced By Love, visit PiercedByLove.com. You can request Rhonda as a speaker or set a personal Prophetic Heart Healing/Deliverance session on the contact page. Or, contact us at appointments@piercedbylove.com.

# NOTES

NOTES

---

# NOTES

NOTES

www.ingramcontent.com/pod-product-compliance
Lightning Source LLC
LaVergne TN
LVHW090525110826
845146LV00003B/985

*9798992257823*